A YOUNG EXPLORER'S NEW YORK

Maps of Manhattan

A

Young Explorer's

NEW YORK

MAPS OF MANHATTAN

by Lavinia Faxon

Maps by Alan Price

NEW YORK GRAPHIC SOCIETY, PUBLISHERS, LTD.   GREENWICH, CONNECTICUT 1962

With love for Sissy

Library of Congress Catalog No. 62-19051

Grateful acknowledgment is given to Holt, Rinehart & Winston, Inc., for permission to quote from *A Book of Americans* by Stephen Vincent Benet, and to Philip Rees of the Museum of the City of New York for his assistance in research.

Printed in the United States of America by the Halliday Lithograph Corporation

Designed by Sheila Lynch

A WORD ABOUT NEW YORK AND ABOUT THIS BOOK

New York, New York, is a wonderful town!

Lots of people say "Everybody rushes so in New York and the buildings are so big it scares me!" Everybody *does* rush, it's true. That's because they are in a great hurry to paint the most wonderful pictures and write the most wonderful books and sing the most wonderful songs; or in a hurry to meet the man who will find oil hidden in the Sahara desert or bring back the rarest spices from the Indies.

And the buildings grow taller and taller to make room for everybody. When there's no more room to grow *out,* the city has to grow *up.*

Don't let the skyscrapers fool you. They look like steel and glass giants, but they were dreams before they were buildings. They were dreamed by people, built by people. And people live and work in them.

It's the *people* who make New York a wonderful town. An Irishman, Brendan Behan, wrote: "New York is inhabited by important people. Nobody but important people live there. They all know that.

Everyone in New York knows he is an important person living among other important people."

There is one thing that everyone should know about New York: it isn't a city that just grew from a small town. It's a collection of a hundred small towns lived in by people from a thousand different places. And like people everywhere, they are sentimental. Even behind the severe steel and glass walls of midtown New York lives any pet you can name, from mynah bird to turtle, Siamese cat to puma. (Bloomingdale's even has signs by its escalators asking you to "Please carry your dog.")

Flowers bloom all over town—in the open stalls on Lexington Avenue, in the elegant shops on Madison, and in the wholesale flower markets around 28th Street on Sixth Avenue. And in the windows of apartments and stationery stores you can find long-necked plants rising bravely from avocado seeds.

Listen to New Yorkers talk. Listen to all the different languages and the different accents.

(please turn page)

5

LISTEN to the sounds of the city. The doorman's whistle, the zoom of the jet, the bark of the little tug scolding the great ocean liner into dock, the fire-siren commanding "Get out of my way—I'm coming through!"

Look! Look at the city! In the early morning the streets are quiet and empty except for the night people: the disk jockey going home, the cleaning woman from the office, and the elevator operator hurrying to start his building to work again.

Look at the city on a late afternoon. On a cross street you can see from one end of the island to the other, with all the buildings rosy from the setting sun.

Look at it in the evening, too. Take a bus and get off in the East Seventies. As you walk back downtown you can see the lights in the skyscrapers sparkle against the dark blue sky. And the clouds, as they reflect their light, are always pink in New York at night.

Best of all, play the game called "Objects hidden in plain sight." *You* know—haven't you played it at a birthday party: "Find the green leaf against the green carpet?" Walk by Finchley's on Fifth Avenue. It looks like a men's store, and is, but lift your eyes and you will see King Arthur's tower! Take a second look when you go by the New York Yacht Club on West 44th Street. You will see the fantail windows of a Spanish galleon!

In the crowd on the corner you may see a TV star waving for a cab. Maybe no one but you notices her. People *do* stop to watch a pretty secretary catch a cricket and wrap it carefully in her handkerchief to take home for a pet.

There are eight million people in New York. We would have to make eight million maps to show them all to you.

In this book we have pointed out a few of New York's hundreds of sights and sounds. We have drawn some of the actors of the New York Company. Tuck the book under your arm and discover them for yourself, and then New York will be your wonderful town, too.

HOW TO USE THIS BOOK

SUPPOSE it is your first day in New York, and you have decided already that it is Fifth Avenue that interests you most. If you will read the brief introductions to the two Fifth Avenue maps in this book, you will get an idea of what there *is* to see (and there's lots) and the maps will show you the general area where all these wonderful sights are to be found. But when you want an *exact* address, then you must check with the Index; we didn't want to tire your eyes by adding tiny little numbered addresses to each of the spots indicated on the maps. And since the streets in most areas of New York are numbered (the numbers go up as you walk uptown) we didn't label them all; they follow a regular pattern. You will find you can get along very nicely using this book in the same way with the Central Park maps and the one suggesting a Crosstown walk as well as those for Fifth Avenue.

Downtown and the Village are not laid out like Midtown Manhattan. Being older they are criss-crossed with little streets that go every which way and the system of numbering streets cannot be used here. Your own maps will show you the general location of the wonderful sights in these fascinating areas, but if you are looking for a particular street, you should by all means have a detailed street guide of New York (all stationery stores and many news-stands have these—try the one in your hotel). The maps for On and Off the Island, Around the Island, Ghosts, and Seasonal Attractions illustrate for you the present-day marvels and past history of New York. Your Index is where you will find the wheres, whys, and whens of what you see drawn. And be sure to check the section that follows the maps (just before the Index) for other hints about how to make the most of your exploration of Manhattan.

FIFTH AVENUE

59th to 51st Street

Fᴵꜰᴛʜ Aᴠᴇɴᴜᴇ at 59th Street is always dressed for dancing school—morning, noon, and especially night. The shops are elegant and so are the hotels …the dignified Plaza always wears white gloves. Directly in front of it is the famous Pulitzer Fountain (some New Yorkers in the past have taken midnight dips here—something *not* recommended for your visit).

Upper Fifth Avenue is ready for a party anytime, flags flying and windows sparkling. If you play the window shopping game down Fifth ("I'll take that diamond necklace, I'll take that Danish cat"), your imaginary trunk will be filled before you reach the end of the block.

See all the proud names that stand for clothes as bright and new as tomorrow's jet: Bonwit Teller, Saks, DePinna, and many more. The famous toy shop, F.A.O. Schwarz, is here, and the great book-stores — Scribner, Brentano, Doubleday. Stouffer's runs a restaurant on the very top of 666 Fifth Avenue from which you can see for miles while you eat.

At Fifth and 56th Street, stop to throw a penny in the Steuben pool; the coins are scooped up daily for the *Herald Tribune's* Fresh Air Fund, which sends city boys and girls on country vacations.

Find the dollar sign over one of St. Thomas' church doors—an architect's joke. Inside the church, in the shrine on the north side, is a big book listing the names of members who have served in the armed forces with many familiar New York names among them.

Don't hesitate to look for the strange and wonderful shops on the cross streets off Fifth Avenue. If you remember that New York is like a big waffle iron and Fifth Avenue is its center ridge, you can never really be lost. Just ask "Which direction is Fifth Avenue, please?" and you're home safe.

FIFTH AVENUE

51st to 34th Street

Across the street from the great St. Patrick's Cathedral is Rockefeller Center, where you can do everything except go to school: ice skate from October to May, eat, mail a postcard, get your shoes fixed, see a movie or stroll in a roof garden, watch a broadcast, buy English lavender and French books, or an airline ticket to Cincinnati or Ceylon. (Correction: you *can* go to school in Rockefeller Center! The Berlitz School will teach you almost any language you want to learn). Among the many famous sights here are the flower beds that line the central walk leading up to the skating rink (winter) and outdoor restaurants (summer). There are benches, also, where you can rest.

As you go along down the Avenue, keep an eye out for Wallachs Dog Bar on the east side of the street. It's the New Yorker's *Farmer's Almanac:* when there's water in it, spring is here; no water means winter is on the way.

Near 44th Street (back on the west side of the Avenue) stands an Olivetti typewriter right out in the open. Yes, you *may* write with it—perhaps "I live in Buffalo. I like New York."

Walking further down Fifth will bring you to 42nd Street. Famous Broadway is a couple blocks to your right, and to your left is Grand Central Station and the gleaming buildings of the United Nations. Right in front of you are the proud lions of the main branch of the New York Public Library. They guard the four million books (some of them in the fine Children's Room). Behind the library is Bryant Park, a good place to stop a moment on a summer noon and listen to a recorded concert; the ice cream man is usually there, too.

A few more blocks brings you to more great stores, Lord and Taylor and B. Altman among them.

Then suddenly, you see the king of buildings, the Empire State!

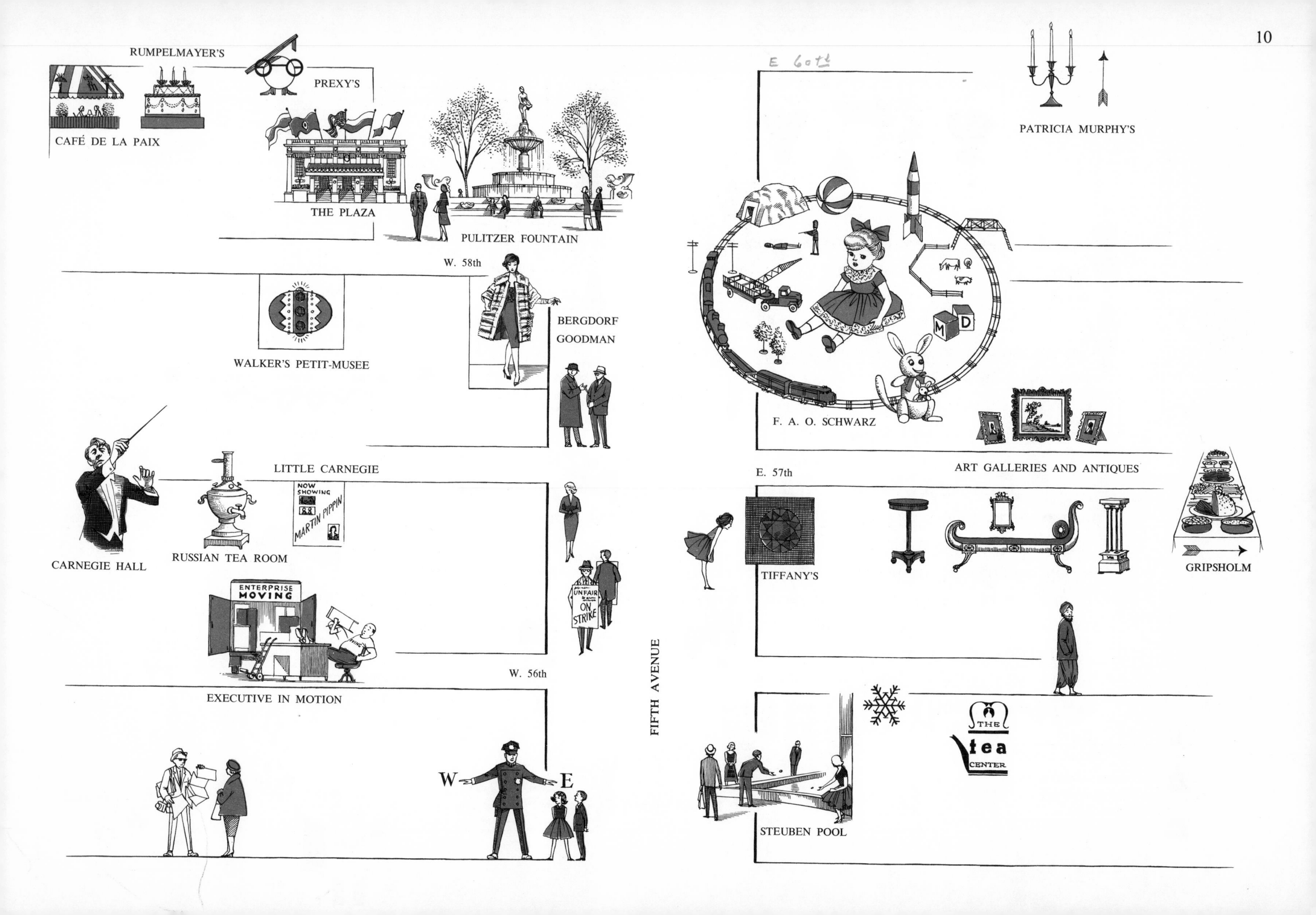

RUMPELMAYER'S

PREXY'S

CAFÉ DE LA PAIX

THE PLAZA

PULITZER FOUNTAIN

E 60th

PATRICIA MURPHY'S

W. 58th

BERGDORF GOODMAN

WALKER'S PETIT-MUSEE

F. A. O. SCHWARZ

LITTLE CARNEGIE

E. 57th

ART GALLERIES AND ANTIQUES

NOW SHOWING MARTIN PIPPIN

CARNEGIE HALL

RUSSIAN TEA ROOM

TIFFANY'S

GRIPSHOLM

ENTERPRISE MOVING

UNFAIR ON STRIKE

W. 56th

EXECUTIVE IN MOTION

FIFTH AVENUE

STEUBEN POOL

THE tea CENTER

W E

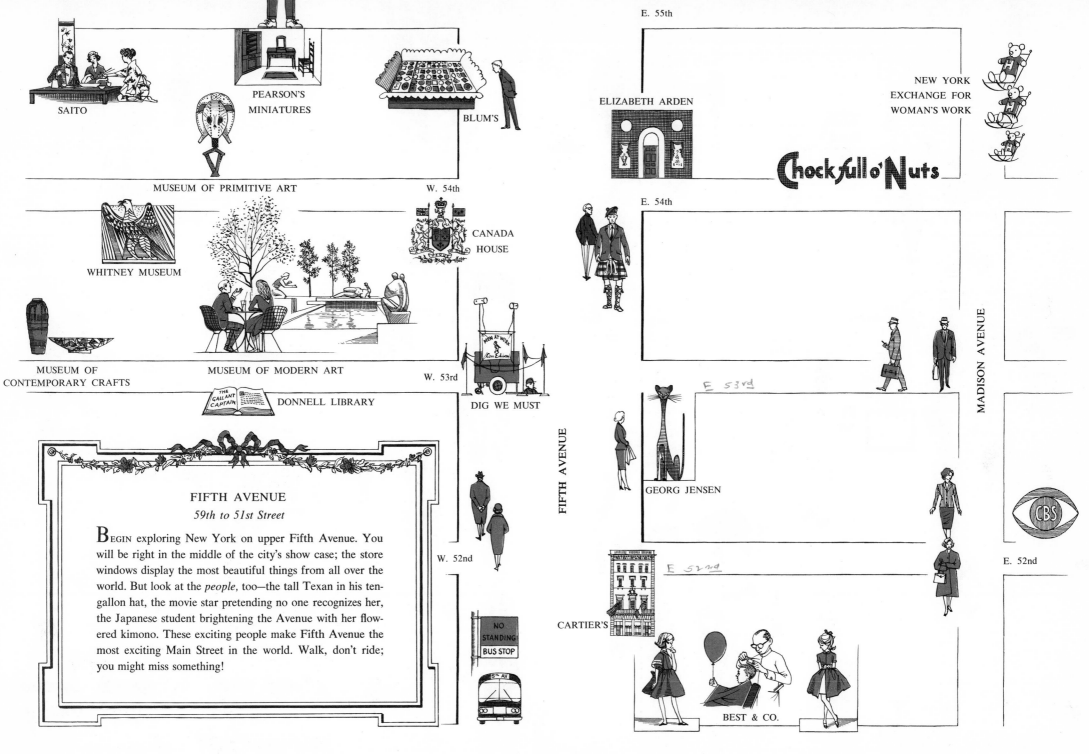

SAITO

PEARSON'S MINIATURES

BLUM'S

MUSEUM OF PRIMITIVE ART

W. 54th

WHITNEY MUSEUM

CANADA HOUSE

MUSEUM OF CONTEMPORARY CRAFTS

MUSEUM OF MODERN ART

W. 53rd

DONNELL LIBRARY

DIG WE MUST

THE GALLANT CAPTAIN

MEN AT WORK

FIFTH AVENUE
59th to 51st Street

BEGIN exploring New York on upper Fifth Avenue. You will be right in the middle of the city's show case; the store windows display the most beautiful things from all over the world. But look at the *people*, too—the tall Texan in his ten-gallon hat, the movie star pretending no one recognizes her, the Japanese student brightening the Avenue with her flowered kimono. These exciting people make Fifth Avenue the most exciting Main Street in the world. Walk, don't ride; you might miss something!

W. 52nd

NO STANDING BUS STOP

5th AV

E. 55th

NEW YORK EXCHANGE FOR WOMAN'S WORK

ELIZABETH ARDEN

Chock full o' Nuts

E. 54th

MADISON AVENUE

FIFTH AVENUE

E. 53rd

GEORG JENSEN

CBS

E. 52nd

CARTIER'S

E. 52nd

BEST & CO.

11

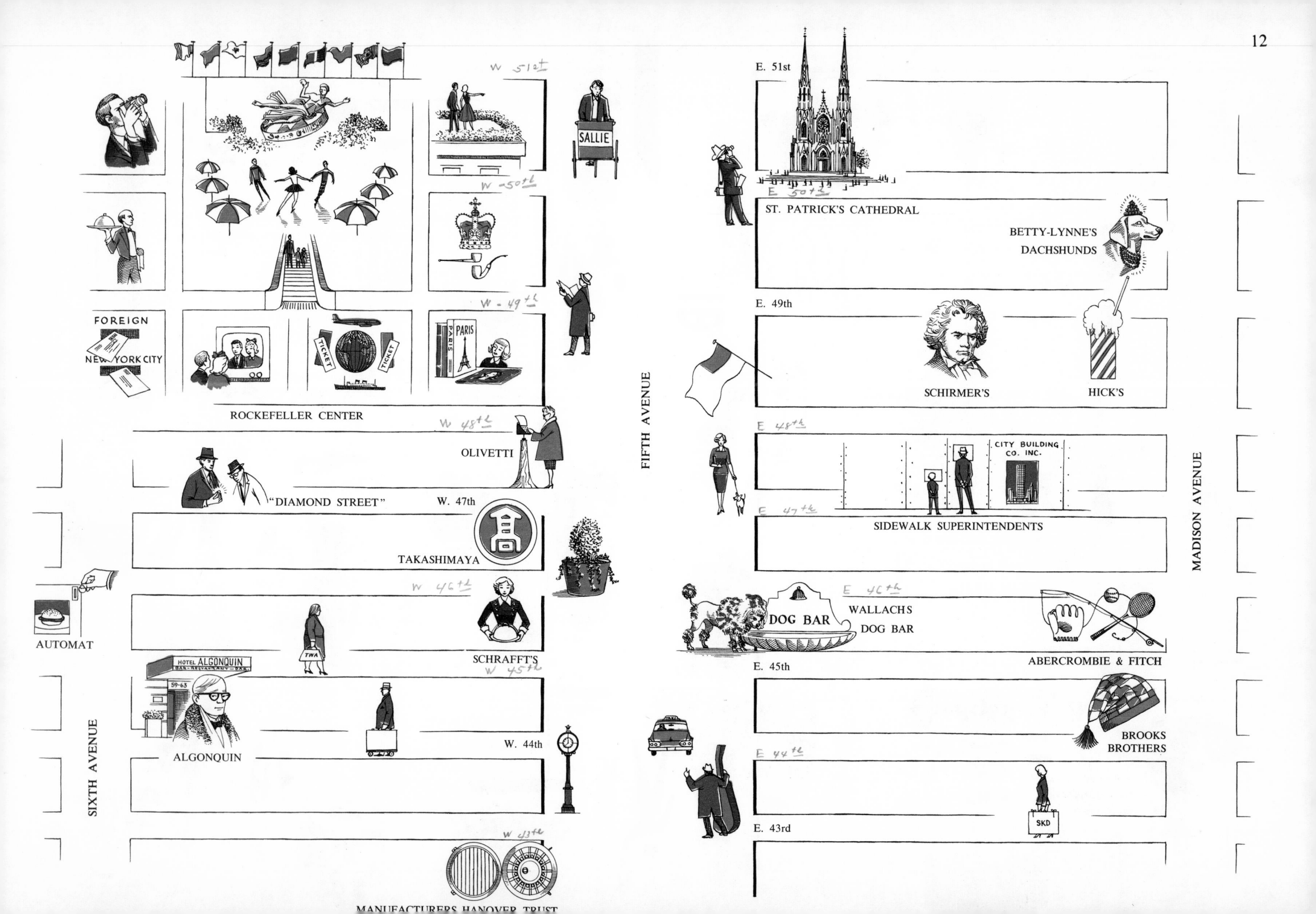

W. 51st

SALLIE

W. 50th

W. 49th

FOREIGN

NEW YORK CITY

PARIS

PARIS

TICKET

TICKET

ROCKEFELLER CENTER

W. 48th

OLIVETTI

"DIAMOND STREET"   W. 47th

TAKASHIMAYA

W. 46th

AUTOMAT

SCHRAFFT'S

HOTEL ALGONQUIN
BAR · RESTAURANT · BAR

59-63

TWA

W. 45th

ALGONQUIN

W. 44th

SIXTH AVENUE

W. 43rd

MANUFACTURERS HANOVER TRUST

FIFTH AVENUE

E. 51st

E. 50th

ST. PATRICK'S CATHEDRAL

BETTY-LYNNE'S

DACHSHUNDS

E. 49th

SCHIRMER'S   HICK'S

E. 48th

CITY BUILDING CO. INC.

E. 47th

SIDEWALK SUPERINTENDENTS

E. 46th

WALLACHS
DOG BAR
DOG BAR

ABERCROMBIE & FITCH

E. 45th

BROOKS
BROTHERS

E. 44th

SKD

E. 43rd

MADISON AVENUE

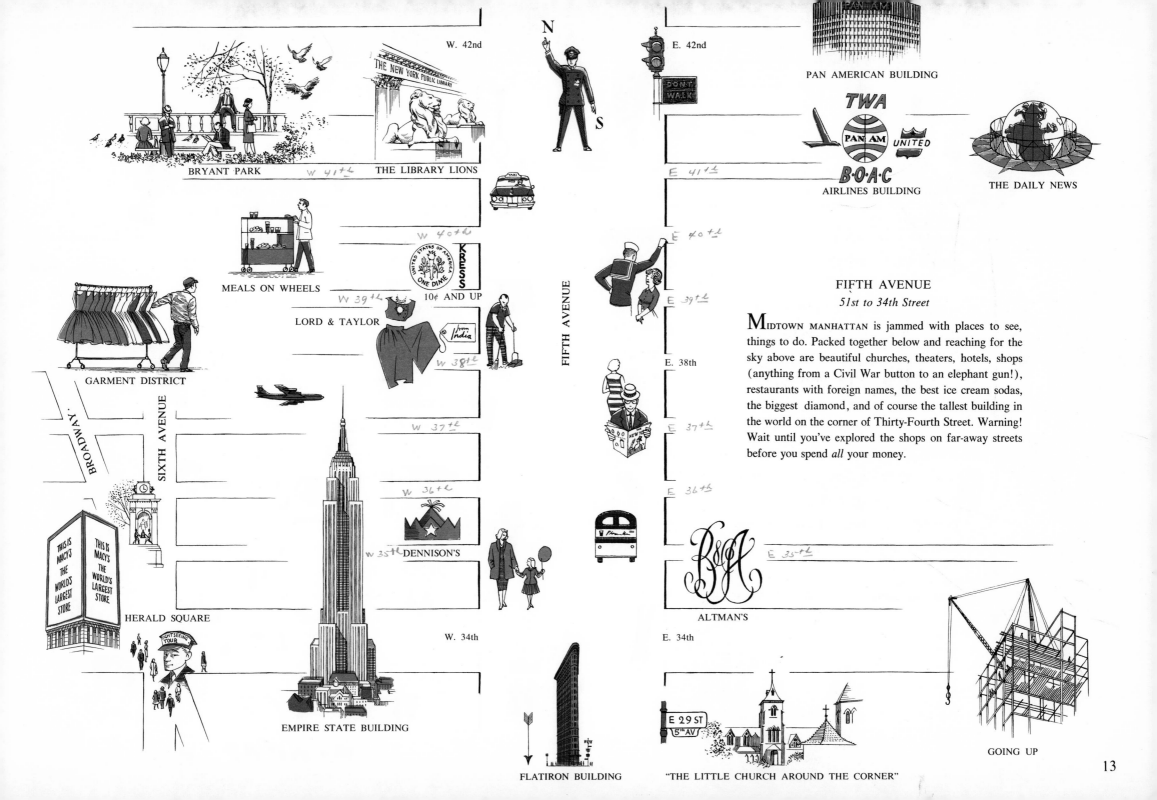

W. 42nd

N
S

E. 42nd

PAN AMERICAN BUILDING

THE NEW YORK PUBLIC LIBRARY

TWA
PAN AM
UNITED
B·O·A·C
AIRLINES BUILDING

THE DAILY NEWS

BRYANT PARK   W. 41st   THE LIBRARY LIONS

E. 41st

TAXI

FIFTH AVENUE

MEALS ON WHEELS   W. 40th

E. 40th

KRESS
UNITED STATES OF AMERICA
ONE DIME
10¢ AND UP

E. 39th

LORD & TAYLOR   W. 39th

from India

W. 38th

E. 38th

FIFTH AVENUE
51st to 34th Street

MIDTOWN MANHATTAN is jammed with places to see, things to do. Packed together below and reaching for the sky above are beautiful churches, theaters, hotels, shops (anything from a Civil War button to an elephant gun!), restaurants with foreign names, the best ice cream sodas, the biggest diamond, and of course the tallest building in the world on the corner of Thirty-Fourth Street. Warning! Wait until you've explored the shops on far-away streets before you spend *all* your money.

GARMENT DISTRICT

BROADWAY

SIXTH AVENUE

W. 37th

E. 37th

W. 36th

E. 36th

THIS IS MACY'S THE WORLD'S LARGEST STORE
THIS IS MACY'S THE WORLD'S LARGEST STORE

W. 35th   DENNISON'S

E. 35th

B&A

ALTMAN'S

HERALD SQUARE

W. 34th

E. 34th

SIGHTSEEING TOUR

EMPIRE STATE BUILDING

E 29 ST
5th AV

GOING UP

FLATIRON BUILDING

"THE LITTLE CHURCH AROUND THE CORNER"

13

CENTRAL PARK

59th to 76th Street

BEFORE you go into the Park, take a look at General Sherman's horse. Did you know that when a soldier's horse has both front hoofs off the ground it means the rider died in battle? That if one hoof is off the ground he died of wounds? That if all four are *on* the ground he died in bed?

You might stop to pat one of the real horses who wait with their carriages on 59th Street, and maybe ask your parents if you can take a ride. The driver will let you sit up on the box with him.

When the carriage brings you back to the Plaza, walk north on the path nearest Fifth Avenue. The first thing you will see is the pony ride, and then you go straight into the Zoo. It isn't a big one, but it has everything a zoo needs: an elephant, a monkey house, a baby hippopotamus, birds and bears. And seals! They have lunch at 1:30 and how they bark and clap their flippers!

Better pick up your balloon here, and a bag of peanuts. The park pigeons are always hungry, and you may see some squirrels.

Beyond this Zoo is a separate one for smaller explorers. You can hold a rabbit in your hands and visit the houses of the Three Little Pigs. Go on to the carousel and reach for a gold ring. Find the Conservatory Pond where toy sailboats race. (Stuart Little sailed one to victory there against great odds, you will remember).

Look for the statues of Hans Christian Andersen and Alice in Wonderland. You can climb over them, and listen to story tellers nearby in the summer. Fish in the big lake if you're not sixteen yet — or take a boat ride.

The Mall is great for roller skating and many evenings you can listen to music there and eat ice cream.

There are hills to climb, ducks to feed, and always —people to watch.

CENTRAL PARK

76th to 104th Street

CENTRAL PARK is fun, summer or winter. In summer, there are flowers to see in the Conservatory Garden and in the Shakespeare Garden. There is baseball to watch (stars from Broadway steal bases Thursday afternoons in summer), and Shakespeare plays on fair evenings: brave kings, lovely princesses, cowards and murderers.

In winter you can skate, ski, or toboggan on Cedar Hill. When the wind blows too hard even to run around the Reservoir, visit one of the museums nearby. But remember that museums are like big cakes. Eat too much and you never want to see a cake again. Take one slice, eat it slowly, and you will want another piece. Take the Metropolitan, for example. It's *enormous!* Go in and just visit the Egyptian tomb and the mummies and then go out and feed a squirrel. Another day, look at the knights' armor, or the costumes of other days. Then lunch by the fountains inside and afterwards go to the Junior Museum and see the exhibits through peepholes.

On the other side of the Park is the New York Historical Society. A sailing ship is there—and carriages old New Yorkers drove through the Park. Nearby is the Hayden Planetarium where you can look up at the oldest star and the youngest satellite. Next to it is the American Museum of Natural History with a sixty million-year-old dinosaur egg, and a seventy-foot whale!

There is one museum you will want to spend hours in because so many displays have been made especially for you. This is the Museum of the City of New York at Fifth Avenue and 104th Street, a delightful picture book of New York's past: portraits, costumes and dioramas show you New Yorkers of other days. There are old doll-houses, old fire engines and whole room of old things with a sign saying "Please Touch."

Please note that on this map we have moved Upper Fifth Avenue far into the page to show you the exciting places to explore on the Avenue by the Park.

W. 76th

W. 74th

W. 72nd

CENTRAL PARK WEST

PICNICKING

ALICE IN WONDERLAND

REFRESHMENTS

HANS CHRISTIAN ANDERSEN

CONSERVATORY POND

THE LAKE

A TOWN HOUSE

PILGRIM STATUE

BETHESDA FOUNTAIN

DANIEL WEBSTER

THE MALL

BALTO STATUE

FRICK MUSEUM

FIFTH AVENUE

E. 76th

E. 72nd

E. 70th

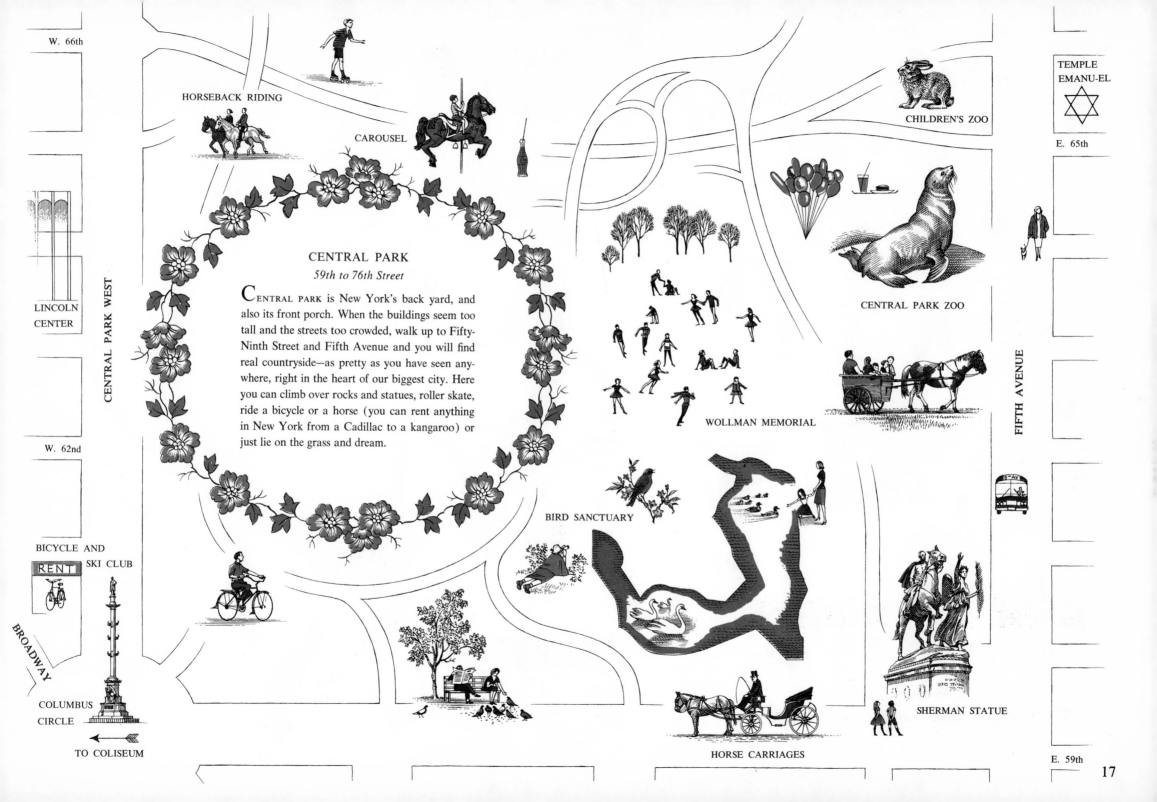

HORSEBACK RIDING

CAROUSEL

CHILDREN'S ZOO

TEMPLE EMANU-EL

E. 65th

CENTRAL PARK
59th to 76th Street

CENTRAL PARK is New York's back yard, and also its front porch. When the buildings seem too tall and the streets too crowded, walk up to Fifty-Ninth Street and Fifth Avenue and you will find real countryside—as pretty as you have seen anywhere, right in the heart of our biggest city. Here you can climb over rocks and statues, roller skate, ride a bicycle or a horse (you can rent anything in New York from a Cadillac to a kangaroo) or just lie on the grass and dream.

CENTRAL PARK ZOO

WOLLMAN MEMORIAL

LINCOLN CENTER

CENTRAL PARK WEST

W. 62nd

FIFTH AVENUE

BIRD SANCTUARY

BICYCLE AND SKI CLUB

RENT

BROADWAY

COLUMBUS CIRCLE

TO COLISEUM

SHERMAN STATUE

HORSE CARRIAGES

E. 59th

TENNIS COURTS

CONSERVATORY GARDENS

E. 103rd MUSEUM OF THE CITY OF NEW YORK

FIFTH AVENUE

E. 94th

AUDUBON SOCIETY

E. 92nd

JEWISH MUSEUM

NEW YORKERS AT HOME

E. 89th

GUGGENHEIM MUSEUM

CENTRAL PARK
76th to 110th Street

Central park is mainly for sunny days. In summer, go boating or fishing, or picnicking. In winter, there are all the cold weather sports to be enjoyed—skiing, ice skating, and tobogganing. For rainy, blowy days, nothing could be better than the museums that ring the Park. They can show you other times and other spheres—dinosaurs and satellites to your left as you look north, mummies and Victorian doll houses to your right. And in all seasons and all weathers, there are the zoos shown on your other map of the Park—the main one and the new Children's Zoo.

THE RESERVOIR

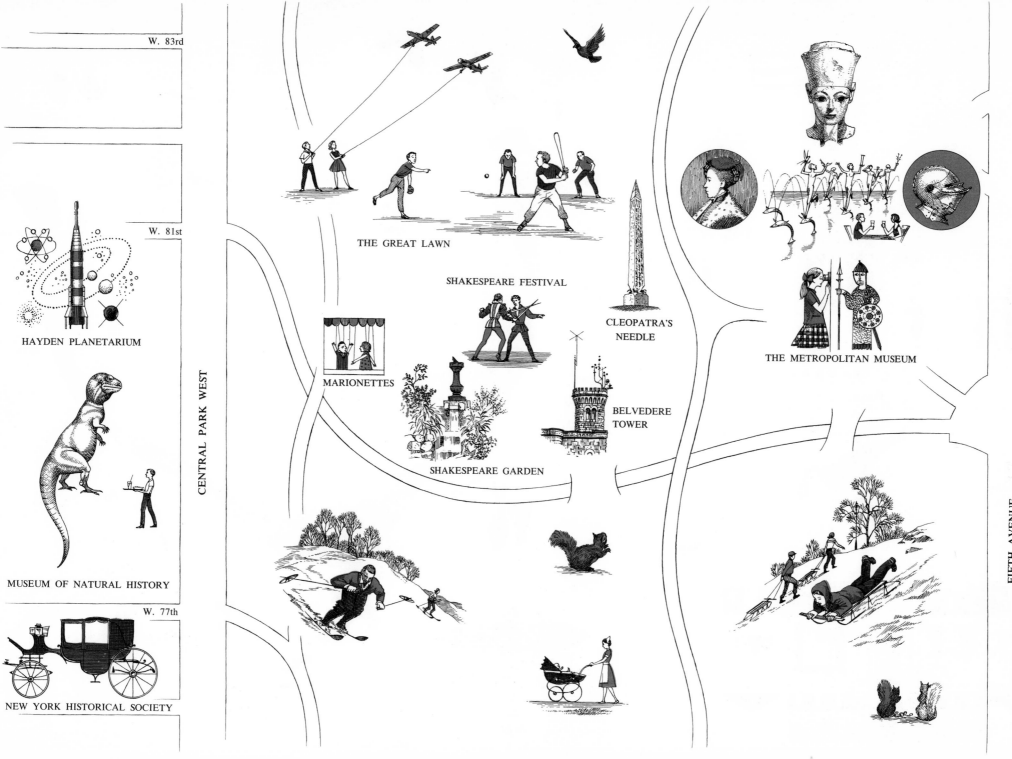

W. 83rd

E. 83rd

W. 81st

HAYDEN PLANETARIUM

CENTRAL PARK WEST

THE GREAT LAWN

SHAKESPEARE FESTIVAL

MARIONETTES

CLEOPATRA'S NEEDLE

THE METROPOLITAN MUSEUM

MUSEUM OF NATURAL HISTORY

SHAKESPEARE GARDEN

BELVEDERE TOWER

E. 79th

W. 77th

NEW YORK HISTORICAL SOCIETY

FIFTH AVENUE

CROSSTOWN

West 50th Street

TAKE a crosstown bus on 49th Street and ride west to the end of the line. There you will see piers where the ocean liners dock, and sometimes battleships and destroyers. Often it is possible to visit both the Navy ships and the commercial liners.

Now get back on the bus at 50th Street for the ride east. You will go by crowded slums for a block or two. New York still has them though they are rapidly being torn down to make room for vast apartment buildings that will be called home by a thousand families.

You will ride by Broadway, a sad and dreary street in the daytime, but at night a tangle of neon lights that give it magic. Look south down Broadway; if your eyes are keen, you may see the news bulletins that race madly around the Times Tower between its third and fourth stories, day and night.

Get off the bus at Sixth Avenue (all New Yorkers call it that, even though the official name is Avenue of the Americas) and sit down for a moment by the fountains of the Time and Life Building. Across the street is Radio City Music Hall where many big movies are first presented and the thirty-six Rockettes dance a straight line like toy soldiers on the Music Hall's huge stage.

Next you will cross Fifth Avenue (with the green light, please. The longest you will have to wait for a light to change anywhere in Manhattan is fifty-four seconds. A police captain said so). From Fifth, with its big stores, walk on to Madison with its smaller ones bursting with enchanting things from far away places.

THEN you reach Park Avenue, Manhattan's most luxurious street. Once it was the avenue of elegant houses and apartments; now it is turning into the Avenue of Glass—banks of glass and glass office buildings.

Walk down to one of the buildings on Park Avenue near Grand Central Station. (Better run—they are tearing them down almost as fast as you can cross the street). Notice the inch of *empty space* between the buildings and the sidewalk. It's called the Safety Inch, and the builders put it there so the windows won't rattle as the trains rumble through the earth below. Bend down and stick your hand in the space and you'll be able to say "I put my hand under a skyscraper!"

Check the flag flying over the door of the Waldorf-Astoria Hotel. It will tell you which king or prime minister is in town.

When you cross the next avenue, Lexington, 50th Street becomes more neighborly again, and you find a shoe repair shop and a Chinese laundry side by side.

Now comes Third Avenue with its antique shops (we are back to the numbered Avenues again, but don't waste your time looking for Fourth Avenue; there isn't one in midtown Manhattan). Here also the brownstone houses begin to be seen, carefully groomed and cherished between the newer apartment buildings.

Stop to buy an apple at the greengrocers on the corner of Second Avenue, then walk to First Avenue and look downtown at the United Nations and the huge Con Edison smokestacks.

Walk to the river and see the fine houses by it. You'll discover their hidden gardens when you take the boat trip around the island.

And now you've gone all the way from west to east. Don't get ambitious and try to walk from south to north unless you are *very* strong. Manhattan is shaped rather like a fish—and it's a very *long* fish (twelve miles from its head to its tail).

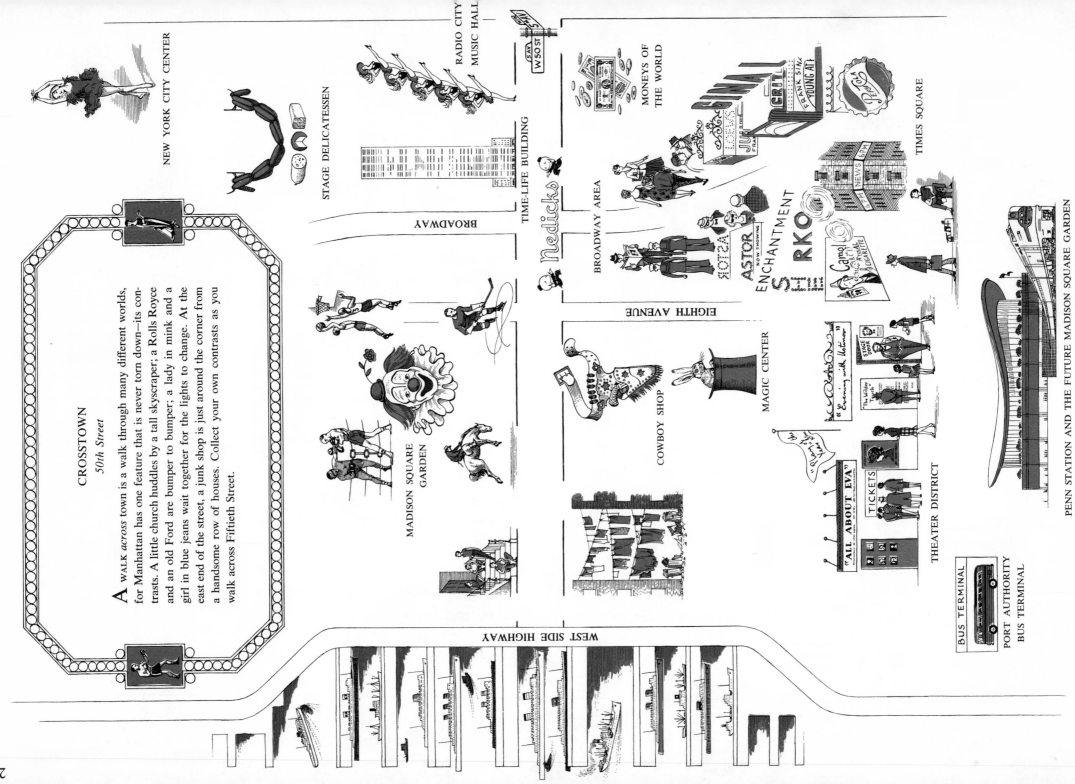

NEW YORK CITY CENTER

STAGE DELICATESSEN

RADIO CITY
MUSIC HALL

TIME-LIFE BUILDING

MONEYS OF
THE WORLD

BROADWAY

BROADWAY AREA

Nedicks

TIMES SQUARE

EIGHTH AVENUE

MADISON SQUARE GARDEN

COWBOY SHOP

MAGIC CENTER

THEATER DISTRICT

PENN STATION AND THE FUTURE MADISON SQUARE GARDEN

"ALL ABOUT EVA"

TICKETS

BUS TERMINAL

PORT AUTHORITY
BUS TERMINAL

WEST SIDE HIGHWAY

CROSSTOWN

50th Street

A WALK *across* town is a walk through many different worlds, for Manhattan has one feature that is never torn down—its contrasts. A little church huddles by a tall skyscraper; a Rolls Royce and an old Ford are bumper to bumper; a lady in mink and a girl in blue jeans wait together for the lights to change. At the east end of the street, a junk shop is just around the corner from a handsome row of houses. Collect your own contrasts as you walk across Fiftieth Street.

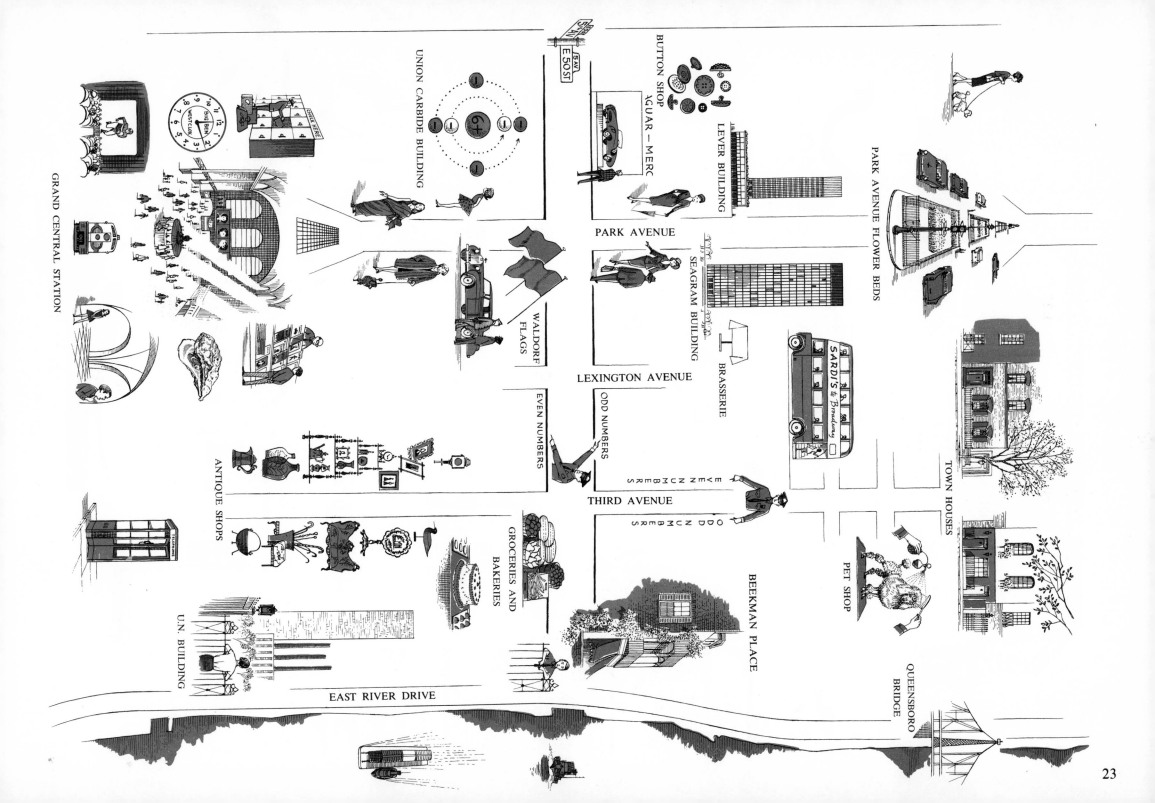

GRAND CENTRAL STATION

UNION CARBIDE BUILDING

BUTTON SHOP

JAGUAR — MERC

LEVER BUILDING

PARK AVENUE FLOWER BEDS

PARK AVENUE

WALDORF FLAGS

SEAGRAM BUILDING

BRASSERIE

LEXINGTON AVENUE

EVEN NUMBERS

ODD NUMBERS

SARDI'S to Broadway

TOWN HOUSES

ANTIQUE SHOPS

THIRD AVENUE

GROCERIES AND BAKERIES

BEEKMAN PLACE

PET SHOP

U.N. BUILDING

EAST RIVER DRIVE

QUEENSBORO BRIDGE

CHECK HERE

BIG BEN WESTCLOX

TELEPHONE

5 AV E 50 ST

THE VILLAGE

At the far south end of Fifth Avenue is Washington Square. Long ago it was a marsh where Indians hunted turkey and later it became a parade ground, then a dueling place. In the northwest corner of the park there still stands a tall oak called "The Hanging Tree."

The place is quieter nowadays: old men play chess, mothers push baby carriages, children wade in the pool, and young and old gather to sing and talk and talk and talk.

Walk north on MacDougal Street where Louisa May Alcott wrote "Little Women" to the Main Street of Greenwich Village: 8th Street. It's a great place for window shopping: handmade shoes, handmade jewelry, Mexican toys (and jumping beans in season), wild clothes—and Stuff. There's a sign in a window on Greenwich Avenue that says STUFF!

Find Gay Street, the shortest in Manhattan. It will take looking for because the streets down here follow the old paths and criss-cross each other.

Find 75½ Bedford Street, the narrowest house in Manhattan, where the poet Edna St. Vincent Millay once lived.

Don't miss Washington Mews, a quiet world of doll houses. These little buildings were once the coach houses of the proud mansions you see on Washington Square.

When you walk up Fifth Avenue you will pass—in spring and summer—the sidewalk cafes and the First Presbyterian Church, with the greenest grass in New York.

Take a minute more to find Gramercy Park six blocks above 14th Street and one block east of Fifth Avenue. You can almost hear the wheels of the hansoms as they circle the pretty park, and the swish of satin as the ladies go up the steps of the lovely old houses—many of them still there.

Don't start exploring the Village too early—many shops don't open until noon. And don't hurry once you're there; it's a neighborhood for lazy exploring.

DOWNTOWN

IF you have already popped into the New York Historical Society and the Museum of the City of New York, the names of many old streets and places down here will be familiar to you. It's a mixed-up part of town. Stenographers eat lunch by Alexander Hamilton's grave. A statue of George Washington stands on the spot where he was inaugurated first President of the United States. He looks down on narrow streets crowded with investment men talking about jet plane stocks. The Federal Reserve Bank, richest in the world, has a bagel cart in front of it.

Look for the clock *in* the sidewalk at Broadway and Maiden Lane—and for the buttonwood tree by the Stock Exchange, kept there in memory of the Dutch burghers who stood under other buttonwood trees long ago and founded the Exchange.

Broadway, which is all business here, is the oldest and longest street on the island (and surely in the state!). From its beginning at the Battery, it goes all the way up to the State House steps in Albany.

Any narrow street will lead you to water and ships. Watch for names that sound like the sea—Seaman's Bank for Savings, The Maritime Company, and of course the Fulton Fish Market. (Be sure to wear rubbers when you go *there*).

Farther north is City Hall with Foley Square nearby where all the courts and judges are. North of Foley Square you will hear so many languages spoken you'll think you need a passport. Here are Orchard and Canal Streets, crowded with push-carts and people buying, selling and—most of all—bargaining.

Close by is Chinatown, only a few crowded blocks in all. On Sundays and holidays the Chinese from all over New York come here to buy sharks' fins and water lily roots, get their mail and visit friends. Be sure to keep some of your New York money to spend here for bright trifles.

VILLAGE PRESBYTERIAN AND
BROTHERHOOD SYNAGOGUE

W 13 ST

FIRST PRESBYTERIAN CHURCH

SPANISH PORTUGUESE
SYNAGOGUE CEMETERY

W. 10th

PATCHIN PLACE

SIDEWALK CAFÉ

STARK-VALLA EMPORIUM

PAPERBACKS

BOOKS

SIXTH AVENUE

W. 8th

JUMBLE SHOP
RESTAURANT
TAP ROOM

JUMBLE SHOP
ON MACDOUGAL ALLEY

GAY STREET

WASHINGTON SQUARE NORTH

S. KLEIN
ON THE
SQUARE

LUCHOW'S

E 14 ST

KLEIN'S (SHOPPING)
AND LUCHOW'S (EATING) ON UNION SQUARE

SALMAGUNDI'S
GAS LIGHTS

E. 11th

AUCTION
TODAY

AUCTIONS

FREE GREENWICH VILLAGE TOUR

ALBERT'S SIGHTSEEING BUS

The
Cricket
Theatre

NOW
SHOWING

PETER and
the WOLF

E 10 ST

2nd AV

TEAKWOOD HOUSE

CHILDREN'S THEATERS ARE
HERE AND ALL OVER

E. 9th

FIFTH AVENUE

E. 8th

BMT
LINES

DOWNTOWN
BROOKLYN

SCHULTE

BOOKS 35¢

20%
SALE

WASHINGTON MEWS

SECONDHAND BOOKSTORES

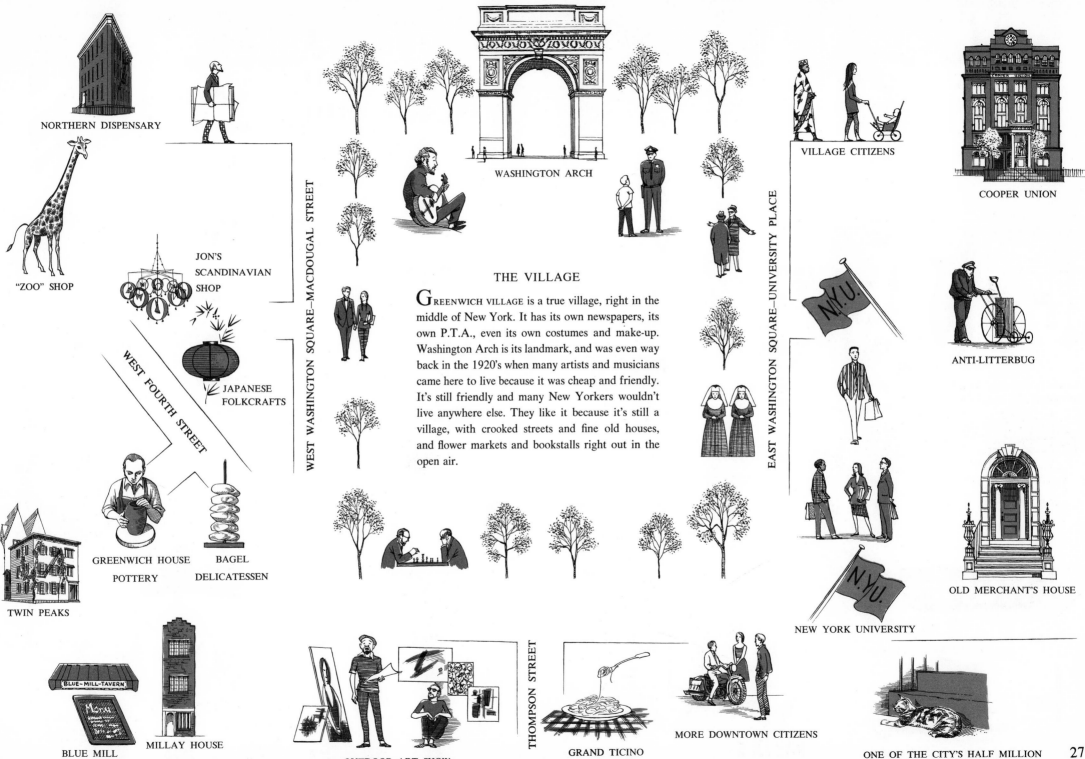

NORTHERN DISPENSARY

"ZOO" SHOP

JON'S SCANDINAVIAN SHOP

JAPANESE FOLKCRAFTS

WEST WASHINGTON SQUARE–MACDOUGAL STREET

WEST FOURTH STREET

GREENWICH HOUSE POTTERY

BAGEL DELICATESSEN

TWIN PEAKS

BLUE MILL

MILLAY HOUSE

OUTDOOR ART SHOW

THOMPSON STREET

GRAND TICINO

WASHINGTON ARCH

THE VILLAGE

Greenwich village is a true village, right in the middle of New York. It has its own newspapers, its own P.T.A., even its own costumes and make-up. Washington Arch is its landmark, and was even way back in the 1920's when many artists and musicians came here to live because it was cheap and friendly. It's still friendly and many New Yorkers wouldn't live anywhere else. They like it because it's still a village, with crooked streets and fine old houses, and flower markets and bookstalls right out in the open air.

VILLAGE CITIZENS

COOPER UNION

EAST WASHINGTON SQUARE–UNIVERSITY PLACE

N.Y.U.

ANTI-LITTERBUG

N.Y.U.

NEW YORK UNIVERSITY

OLD MERCHANT'S HOUSE

MORE DOWNTOWN CITIZENS

ONE OF THE CITY'S HALF MILLION

27

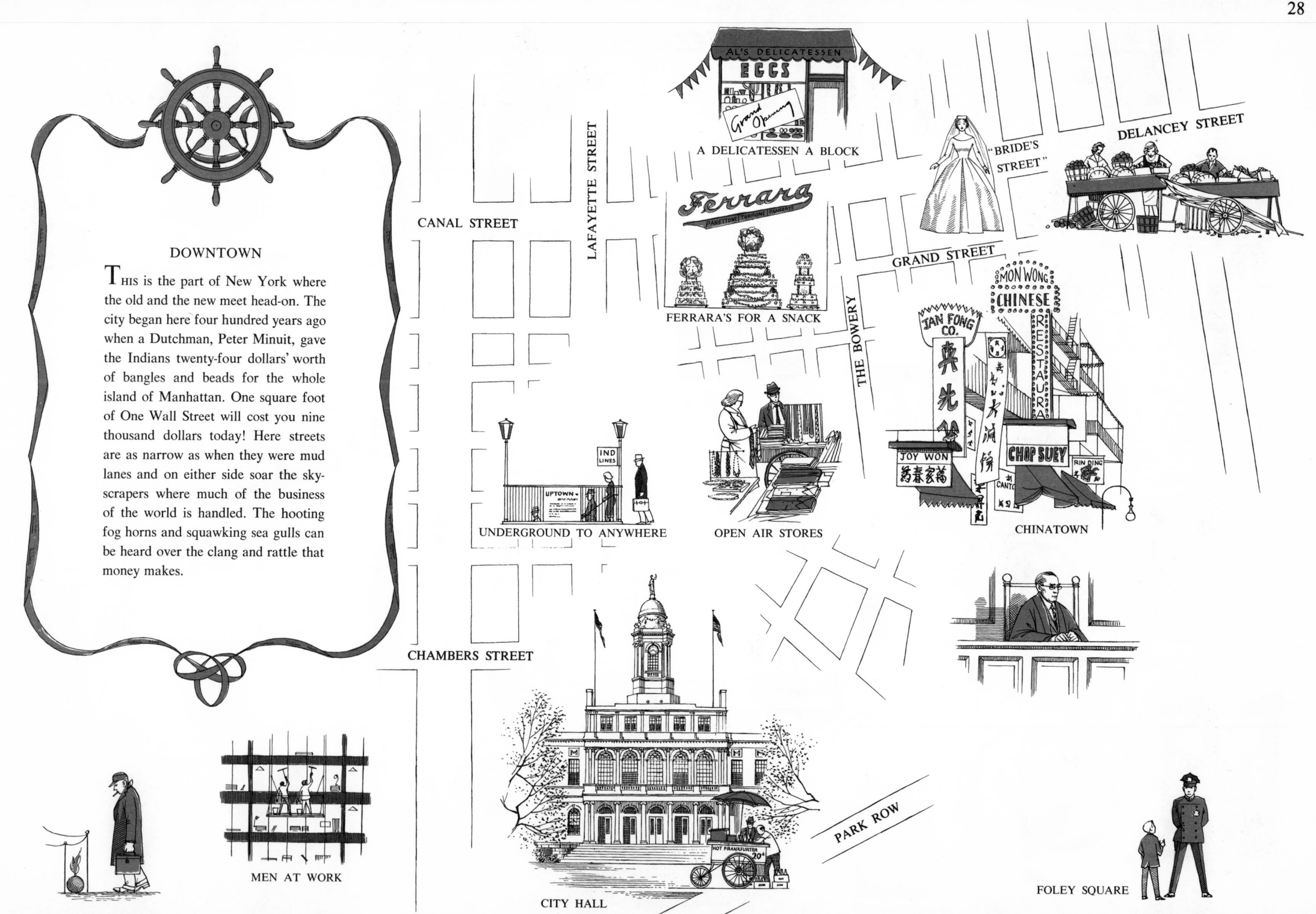

DOWNTOWN

This is the part of New York where the old and the new meet head-on. The city began here four hundred years ago when a Dutchman, Peter Minuit, gave the Indians twenty-four dollars' worth of bangles and beads for the whole island of Manhattan. One square foot of One Wall Street will cost you nine thousand dollars today! Here streets are as narrow as when they were mud lanes and on either side soar the sky-scrapers where much of the business of the world is handled. The hooting fog horns and squawking sea gulls can be heard over the clang and rattle that money makes.

CANAL STREET

LAFAYETTE STREET

AL'S DELICATESSEN

EGGS

Grand Opening

A DELICATESSEN A BLOCK

Ferrara
PANETTONE TORRONE PANFORTE

FERRARA'S FOR A SNACK

GRAND STREET

"BRIDE'S STREET"

DELANCEY STREET

THE BOWERY

MON WONG
CHINESE RESTAURANT
TAN FONG CO.
JOY WON
CHOP SUEY
RIN DING
CANTO

CHINATOWN

IND LINES

UPTOWN

UNDERGROUND TO ANYWHERE

OPEN AIR STORES

CHAMBERS STREET

CITY HALL

HOT FRANKFURTER 20¢

PARK ROW

MEN AT WORK

FOLEY SQUARE

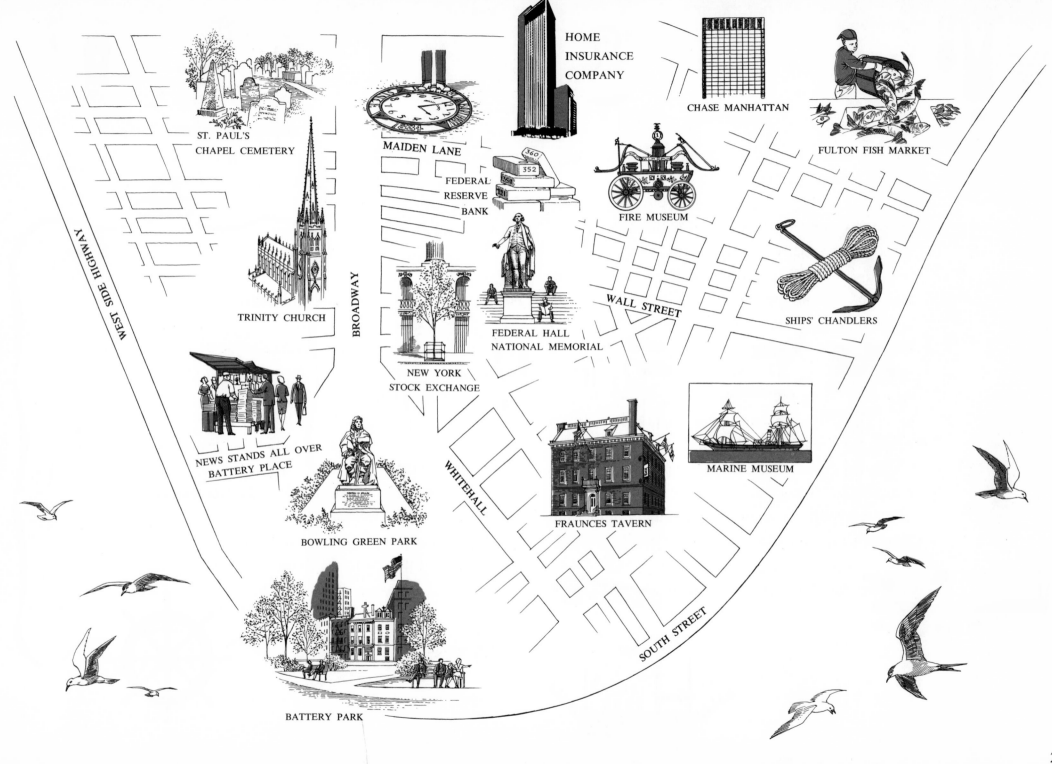

ST. PAUL'S
CHAPEL CEMETERY

MAIDEN LANE

HOME
INSURANCE
COMPANY

CHASE MANHATTAN

FULTON FISH MARKET

FEDERAL
RESERVE
BANK

FIRE MUSEUM

TRINITY CHURCH

BROADWAY

WALL STREET

SHIPS' CHANDLERS

FEDERAL HALL
NATIONAL MEMORIAL

NEW YORK
STOCK EXCHANGE

WEST SIDE HIGHWAY

NEWS STANDS ALL OVER
BATTERY PLACE

MARINE MUSEUM

WHITEHALL

FRAUNCES TAVERN

BOWLING GREEN PARK

SOUTH STREET

BATTERY PARK

ON AND AROUND THE ISLAND

THERE'S no better way to "see New York whole" than to take the boat trip around the island. From the ship's railing, you'll get a view that will make all the pieces of the sprawling city fall into place: the downtown skyscraper canyons, the United Nations, the gardens and balconies of Beekman Place and Sutton Place. You'll see all kinds of ships—from the red fireboat docked at Gracie Mansion, the Mayor's house, to the ocean liners on the Hudson.

By the time you land, you will have a good idea of where to begin your own exploration of the city away from midtown.

Why not take a picnic basket and go up to Inwood Park? Before you have lunch you can dig in the caves for Indian arrowheads.

Do you want to spend an hour in the Middle Ages with knights and their ladies? You can do that by visiting The Cloisters.

Stop at Riverside Church and climb the tower for a gull's-eye view of the broad Hudson and the New Jersey cliffs, and visit Grant's Tomb nearby.

Now cross Riverside Drive and hunt for the Buddhist saint who stands between two tall buildings. If you're not ready for him, he'll give you quite a scare—just as a giant on your front porch would.

Do you like to collect things? New York has a shop for every kind of collector. Shells? Go to McArthur Shell Shop; you'll find shells from Florida to the South Seas. Stamps? Coins? Gimbels has the most varied collection in town. Are you a railroad man? At the Lionel Train Exhibit you'll find every piece of railroad equipment you ever dreamed of, all in miniature!

If you should wake up *very* early one morning, hurry to the corner of Sixth Avenue and West 27th Street to see the prettiest sight in New York: rows and rows of flowers stacked along the street, waiting to light up florists' windows all over town.

OFF THE ISLAND

WOULD you like to land on the tip of the great island just as the first settlers did? Then take the ferry to Staten Island. On the way back, you'll see the fantastic skyline of New York, and you will understand why Queen Elizabeth II said "Whee!" when *she* saw it.

A walk over Brooklyn Bridge and a turn to the right will lead you into the doll-like streets of Brooklyn Heights. If you stroll along the Esplanade there in the early evening, you can look back across the East River and see a city that looks like a huge forest of lighted Christmas trees.

Take the subway to Coney Island—not on weekends or holidays, unless you like being mistaken for a sardine! Stand in the front car of the subway; you'll feel you are riding a dragon! At Coney Island there's everything you can think of: sea, sand, rides, and the most famous hot dogs in the world.

In Queens are the airports, with planes zooming in from all over the world. At Kennedy International Airport, you may visit an animal airport for traveling poodles and panthers.

In the Bronx is the huge zoo where you can ride a camel and, in the Children's Zoo, you can also hold some of the animals (well, not the elephant). Farm-in-the-Zoo has all the barnyard animals you have heard about but maybe never seen, since ordinary zoos don't always have them. Right next door are the Botanical Gardens with tall greenhouses filled with tropical trees and orchids.

And all around are bridges and more bridges. If you have time, walk over some of them. You'll feel like a sea gull as you look down at the river traffic.

Look especially for the path by the Hudson River south of the George Washington Bridge where you can walk under the trees. It's so pretty you'll want to pretend your name is Stuyvesant and stay forever in New Amsterdam.

INWOOD HILL
PARK

HALL OF FAME

HARLEM RIVER

THE CLOISTERS
FORT TRYON PARK

JUMEL MANSION

MUSEUM OF THE
AMERICAN INDIAN

HUDSON RIVER

GRANT'S
TOMB

LEWISOHN STADIUM

RIVERSIDE CHURCH

COLUMBIA
UNIVERSITY

CATHEDRAL OF
ST. JOHN THE DIVINE

BUDDHIST
CHURCH

ON AND AROUND THE ISLAND

THIS map tells two stories: that of the two great rivers that
make Manhattan an island and also about parks and museums to explore that are far from the center of town. It
shows, too, shops tucked around the city where you will find
toys and exhibits that will delight you. You will see some of
these places when you take the boat trip around the island.
The rest you can find by bus or on foot. They can be explored on one of your "please-get-up-Daddy-it's-six-o'clock"
days.

EAST RIVER

CENTRAL PARK
(IN MINIATURE)

A.S.P.C.A.

GRACIE MANSION

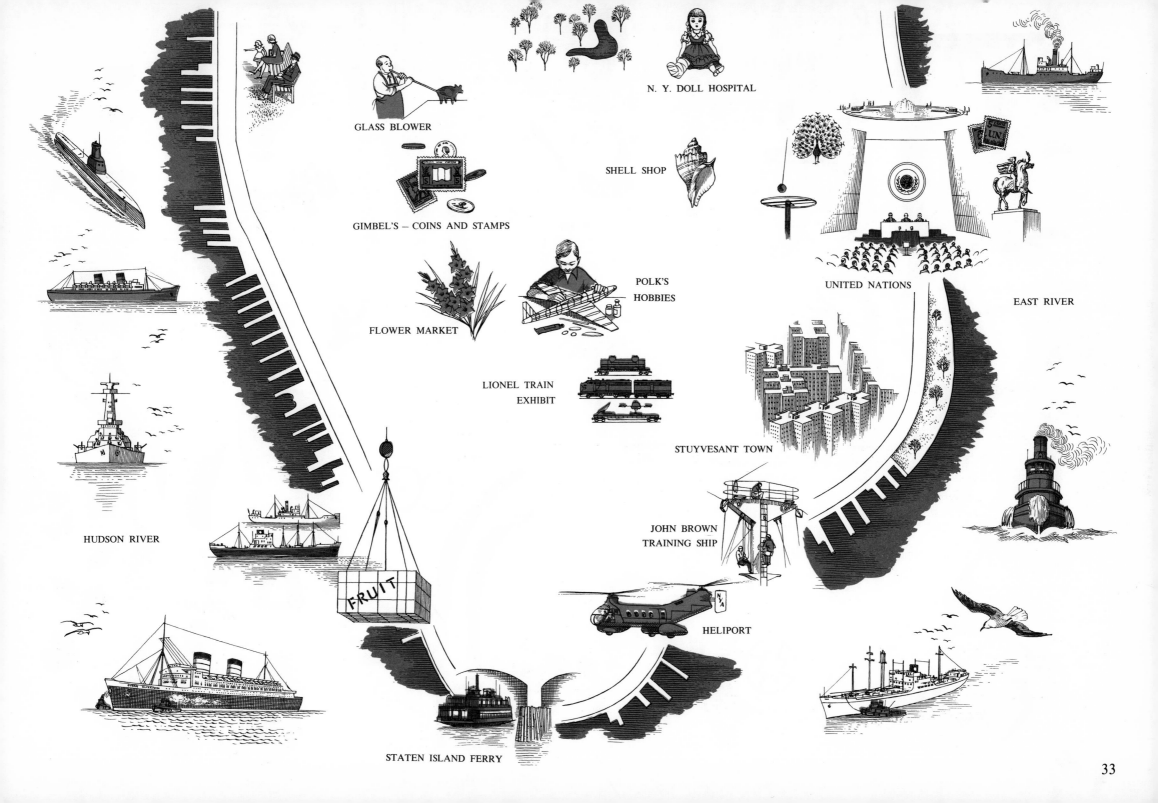

N. Y. DOLL HOSPITAL

GLASS BLOWER

SHELL SHOP

GIMBEL'S — COINS AND STAMPS

POLK'S
HOBBIES

UNITED NATIONS

EAST RIVER

FLOWER MARKET

LIONEL TRAIN
EXHIBIT

STUYVESANT TOWN

HUDSON RIVER

JOHN BROWN
TRAINING SHIP

FRUIT

HELIPORT

STATEN ISLAND FERRY

N. Y. BOTANICAL GARDENS

BRONX ZOO

FREEDOMLAND

BRONX-WHITESTONE BRIDGE

GEORGE WASHINGTON BRIDGE

YANKEE STADIUM

LA GUARDIA AIRPORT

PALISADES PARK

TRIBOROUGH BRIDGE

RANDALL'S ISLAND

OFF THE ISLAND

MANHATTAN is a real island—water on all sides! The East River separates Manhattan from Brooklyn, the Hudson flows between the island and New Jersey, and the Harlem River is the boundary that marks off Manhattan from the Bronx. Riding these waters

QUEENSBOROUGH BRIDGE

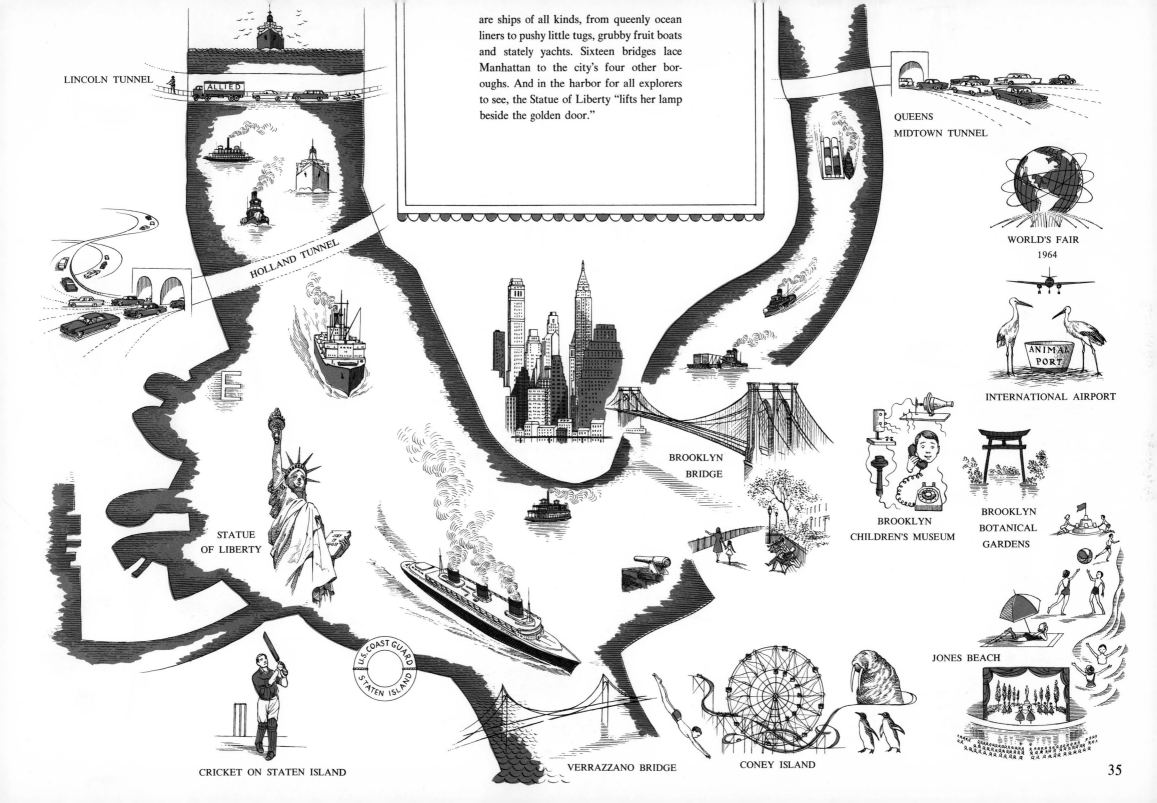

LINCOLN TUNNEL

ALLIED

are ships of all kinds, from queenly ocean liners to pushy little tugs, grubby fruit boats and stately yachts. Sixteen bridges lace Manhattan to the city's four other boroughs. And in the harbor for all explorers to see, the Statue of Liberty "lifts her lamp beside the golden door."

QUEENS
MIDTOWN TUNNEL

HOLLAND TUNNEL

WORLD'S FAIR
1964

INTERNATIONAL AIRPORT

ANIMAL PORT

STATUE
OF LIBERTY

BROOKLYN
BRIDGE

BROOKLYN
CHILDREN'S MUSEUM

BROOKLYN
BOTANICAL
GARDENS

JONES BEACH

U.S. COAST GUARD
STATEN ISLAND

CRICKET ON STATEN ISLAND

VERRAZZANO BRIDGE

CONEY ISLAND

35

WINTER

WE wish we could make a recording of "Jingle Bells" to go with this map. New York glows with Christmas on every street. The delicatessen man takes down the sign that says "No checks cashed—this means YOU" and puts up a tinselled "Merry Christmas" in its place.

The hot chestnut vendors are out on the street; so are the Santa Clauses—on every corner of Fifth Avenue. The whole Avenue sparkles, with the tree of light at Lord and Taylor's and the tallest Christmas tree in the world at Rockefeller Center. The store windows teem with bright clothes and toys; in some, fairy tales are told with moving dolls. The New York City Ballet dances the Nutcracker Ballet at City Center.

All at once the lights go on up and down Park Avenue when the carol singing starts at the Brick Church. (It's a Grimm's fairy tale when the amber lights go on all around the Seagram Building).

And the dignified library lions wear wreaths.

It's a bright, crowded, friendly time in the city. This is one season you can't be lonely even if you try. At Christmas, there are no strangers in New York.

SPRING

NEXT to Christmas, Easter is the most enchanting time to see Manhattan. The town is in flower and people look as if they were going to burst out singing. Well, not *everyone*.

Forests of tulips glow in the middle of Park Avenue. Little girls in white walk by on their way to First Communion; Jewish boys and girls look forward to Passover; Russians and Ukrainians give each other beautiful Easter eggs.

The Flower Show comes to the Coliseum—the Automobile Show, too.

There are street festivals and Coney Island opens for fun.

And there are parades; The biggest one of the year is on the 17th of March, St. Patrick's Day. A green line is painted up the middle of Fifth Avenue and all the policemen put on their white gloves. Bands from nearly every high school and college in and near New York line up on the side streets to join the march and the Cardinal waits on the steps of the Cathedral to bless them as they go by.

And all New Yorkers—Chinese, Polish, Dutch— wear something green and are Irish for one day.

SUMMER

Nᴇᴡ Yᴏʀᴋ goes outdoors in the summer. The very old and the very young go over to the Park or just sit on their own front steps. The in-betweens explore farther away.

Coney Island is the greatest summer playground. After you have gone through the Fun House and eaten a hot dog (they were invented at Coney Island) why not go to the Aquarium to meet Olaf, the friendly seal, and the penguins, dressed for the opera? There are fireworks at Coney every Tuesday night in the summer.

Watch the papers for the schedule of sports events on Randall's Island and for the jazz festival there. Look also for shows in the summer theaters an easy distance from Manhattan; there are several.

This is the time to explore Jones Beach. You can spend a fine summer day there, swimming and picnicking, and in the evening see a play under the stars.

There's Freedomland to find, too, for fun and glimpses of life in all the States in the old days— cowboys and Indians all over the place. And in Manhattan, of all places, you will hear the bell of the Good Humor man in the neighborhood streets.

AUTUMN

Nᴏᴡ what *are* we going to do? We've said Easter and Christmas are wonderful in New York. Summer, too. Now we want to say Autumn is the best. We expect the answer is that there *is* no dull time to explore the town. There are exciting things to do in every season.

Early Autumn has the tennis matches out in nearby Forest Hills, and the World Series is played at Yankee Stadium more often than some people like.

This is when the new plays open—and so does school, even in New York.

Suddenly it's Halloween! Down in Greenwich Village the store owners offer prizes for the best window pictures painted by children. (The older artists again put their pictures around Washington Square earlier in the Autumn. You can have your *own* portrait painted).

Ice skating starts at Wollman Memorial Rink in Central Park and at Rockefeller Center. The men who sell hot roasted chestnuts set up their stands all over town.

And then comes the Christmas season, which officially begins with the gigantic Macy Parade on Thanksgiving Day.

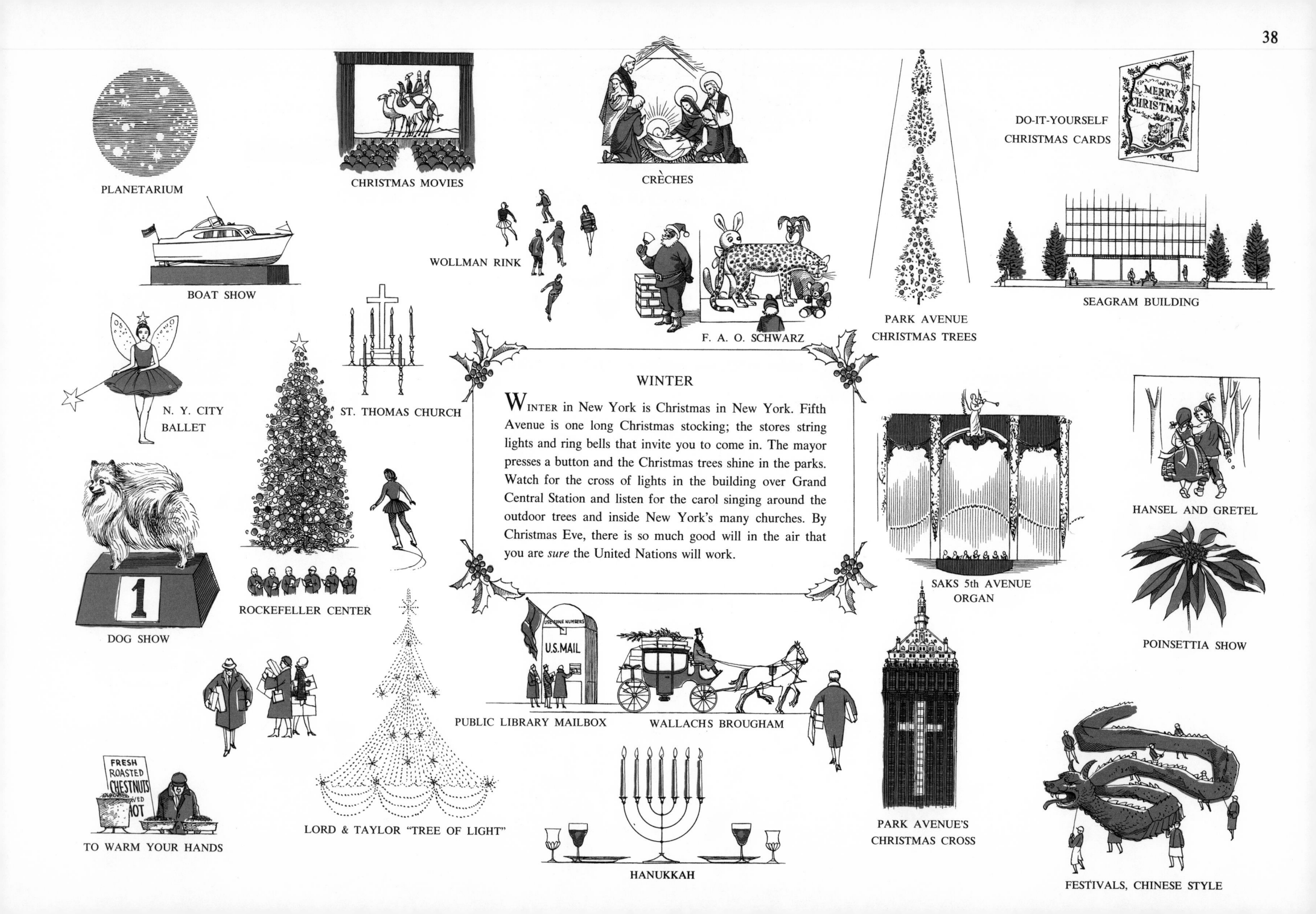

PLANETARIUM

CHRISTMAS MOVIES

CRÈCHES

DO-IT-YOURSELF
CHRISTMAS CARDS

PARK AVENUE
CHRISTMAS TREES

SEAGRAM BUILDING

BOAT SHOW

WOLLMAN RINK

F. A. O. SCHWARZ

N. Y. CITY
BALLET

ST. THOMAS CHURCH

WINTER

Winter in New York is Christmas in New York. Fifth Avenue is one long Christmas stocking; the stores string lights and ring bells that invite you to come in. The mayor presses a button and the Christmas trees shine in the parks. Watch for the cross of lights in the building over Grand Central Station and listen for the carol singing around the outdoor trees and inside New York's many churches. By Christmas Eve, there is so much good will in the air that you are *sure* the United Nations will work.

HANSEL AND GRETEL

SAKS 5th AVENUE
ORGAN

POINSETTIA SHOW

DOG SHOW

ROCKEFELLER CENTER

PUBLIC LIBRARY MAILBOX

WALLACHS BROUGHAM

PARK AVENUE'S
CHRISTMAS CROSS

FRESH
ROASTED
CHESTNUTS

TO WARM YOUR HANDS

LORD & TAYLOR "TREE OF LIGHT"

HANUKKAH

FESTIVALS, CHINESE STYLE

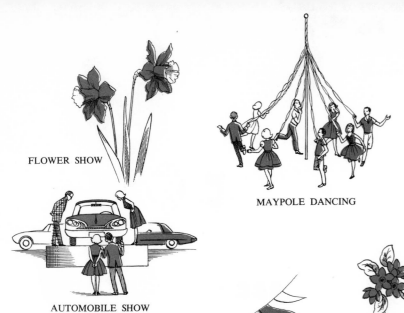

FLOWER SHOW

AUTOMOBILE SHOW

MAYPOLE DANCING

ST. PATRICK'S DAY PARADE

INDOOR POLO

BASEBALL BEGINS

CIRCUS

SPRING

JUST as winter in New York means Christmas, so does spring mean Easter and the beginning again, as it means everywhere. The tulip trees behind St. Patrick's and the tree of heaven in the hidden gardens bloom like Easter candles. (A tree in New York is a miracle and cherished as such). Artists show their paintings around Washington Square, the English-born play cricket on Staten Island, bicycles and roller skates appear in Central Park. And the Circus comes to town!

TULIP TREES
BY ST. PATRICK'S

PARK AVENUE TULIPS

PET SHOW

CRICKET

FLOWER CART

EASTER PARADE

RUSSIAN EASTER

CHERRY BLOSSOM TIME

OUTDOOR ART SHOW

PALISADES PARK

LEWISOHN STADIUM

BASEBALL IN CENTRAL PARK

SHAKESPEARE IN THE PARK

FREEDOMLAND

MODEL BOAT REGATTA

HUDSON BOAT TRIP

FESTIVAL, JAPANESE STYLE

FESTIVAL, PUERTO RICAN STYLE

ROSE FESTIVAL

SUMMER

New york takes off its tie in the summer. The out-of-towners pour in, the New Yorkers (who can) pour out. All day and far into the night, the rest sit on the benches by the rivers, in the parks nearest their homes, and by the fountains that are now all over town. Big Central Park is abloom with people. They listen to the band on the Mall, watch Shakespeare, go boating, or stroll along the walks in the cool of the evening and hum "It's so peaceful in the country."

FIREWORKS

EVERYWHERE

ALL OVER TOWN

STREET CAROUSEL

FESTIVAL, ITALIAN STYLE

SIDEWALK CAFÉ

CONEY ISLAND

JONES BEACH

LINCOLN CENTER

MACY'S THANKSGIVING DAY PARADE

WOLLMAN RINK

P.A.L. HALLOWEEN PARTIES

WORLD SERIES

ICECAPADES

HORSE SHOW

AUTUMN

Now New York comes out of its summer cocoon, a sparkling butterfly. "Its going to be a great season," everybody seems to say as they walk (almost fly) down the avenues. The new plays open, the concerts begin, the shop windows show the shape of things to come; horses gallop and trot, jump and canter at the Horse Show and Gotham ladies wear their newest party dresses and shiniest diamonds to watch them. Benjamin Franklin wouldn't have needed a kite to find the electricity of autumn in New York. The air crackles with it!

STORY TELLING
IN CITY LIBRARIES

FOREST HILLS
CHAMPIONSHIP TENNIS

A FIRST NIGHT

FESTIVAL OF SAN GENNARO

HALLOWEEN IN GREENWICH VILLAGE

PULASKI DAY PARADE

OUTDOOR ARTIST AT WORK

JUNIOR OLYMPICS

41

GHOSTS

Your teacher may frown at us, but here is the history of New York City in a paragraph.

The Indians got here first. (The Algonquins called the island Man-na-hat-ta, "celestial country"). Henry Hudson found them when he sailed up the Hudson River in his ship, *The Half Moon*. The Dutch came next, looking for furs. Then the British arrived, took over the Dutch town of New Amsterdam and named it New York after the Duke of York, brother of their king. They stayed until they were beaten by George Washington, and New York has been American ever since. The city grew and grew until it became the enormous and amazing place it is today.

(It was built by *young* men, by the way—men with children your age and younger. They weren't always as old and stern as they look in the statues you see).

This all took four hundred years. You can find the shadows of those years all over town: the flag of New York City is made up of the colors of the Dutch flag; Wall Street is named for the wall Peter Stuyvesant, an early Dutch Governor, built to keep out the Indians; Pearl Street *was* made of pearls (well, oyster shells once paved it); Maiden Lane was the Lover's Lane of New Amsterdam; the Dutch really bowled on Bowling Green; Coenties Slip *was* a slip, or dock.

NEW YORK was always a port town. Four-masted schooners docked downtown, their masts jutting into the streets. Commodore Cornelius Vanderbilt ran the ferries to Staten Island. Later, he and other men built the railroads that brought more goods and more people to New York.

The ships brought millions of immigrants from Europe to work on the railroads or in the factories that were sprouting up all over the city.

As the town grew bigger, people who could afford to moved uptown—first to Washington Square and Lower Fifth Avenue, later to Upper Fifth Avenue. You can still see some of the brownstone houses they built and a few of their marble palaces still line Central Park. Fifty years ago in Central Park, rich New Yorkers raced the newest invention—the automobile.

The elevator was invented, one of the reasons that made skyscrapers possible. So the magic mountains rose all over town.

A crowded history was written in these four hundred years. Look sharp and you can find the Dutch names on street signs, the three feathers of the Prince of Wales' crest over the pulpit at St. Paul's, and the British crown on the flagpole of Columbia University, which was once called King's College. You can still see the cottage where Poe wrote "The Raven," and Cooper Union, too, where a young lawyer from Illinois delivered a speech that did much to make him President Lincoln. You can also still visit the house of Theodore Roosevelt—President, Governor, Rough Rider and big game hunter.

If you shut your eyes you may hear, over the traffic noises, the jingle of bells as the sleighs race up a quieter Fifth Avenue on an earlier snowy New York morning.

44

HUDSON RIVER

THE PALISADES

INWOOD PARK

INDIAN CANOES

BRITISH REDCOATS

CLERMONT

THE KNICKERBOCKERS

AMERICA'S CUP RACES

EARLY
DUTCH HOUSE

EAST RIVER

GHOSTS

New York City is alive with history and haunted by ghosts!
Look there! Mrs. Murray in her parlor on Murray Hill pours
tea for a British officer, delaying him just long enough to
allow General Putnam to escape up the island. And down
near the East River they are hanging Nathan Hale. Farther
downtown, old Peter Stuyvesant thumps around his farmyard
on his silver-ringed wooden leg.

"And just remember this about
Our ancestors so dear;
They didn't find an empty land,
The Indians were here."

"THE EL"

WINTER SPORTS
A HUNDRED YEARS AGO

AUTO RACES

GENERAL STEUBEN

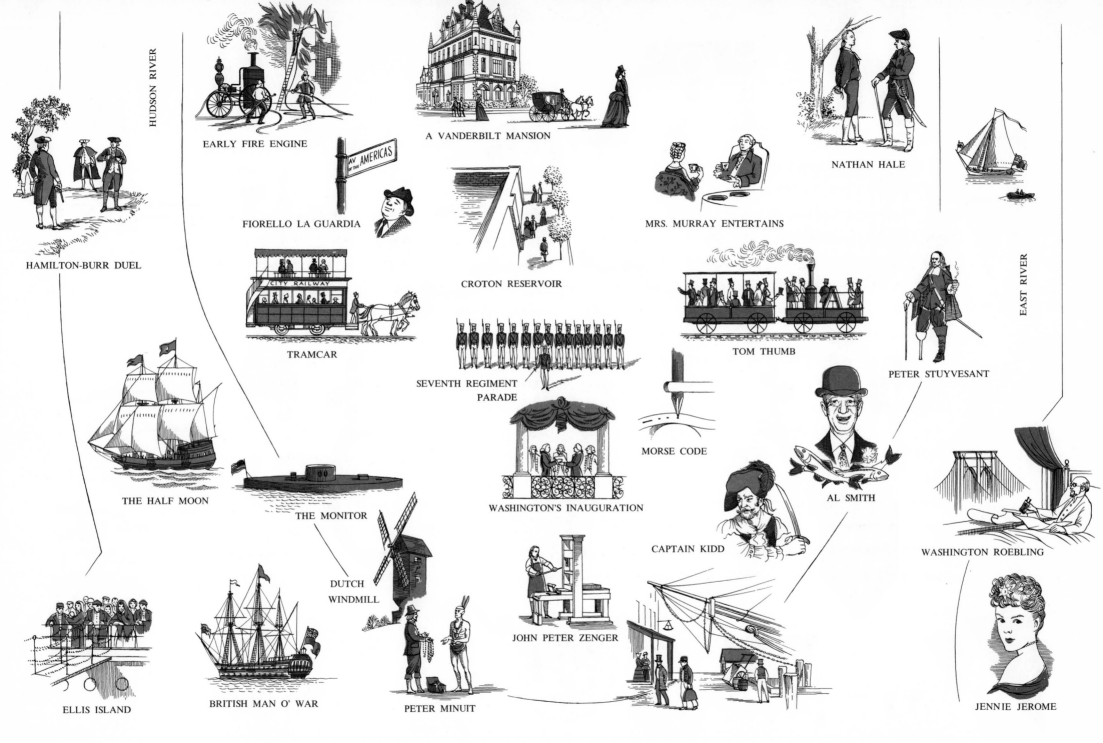

HUDSON RIVER

EARLY FIRE ENGINE

A VANDERBILT MANSION

NATHAN HALE

HAMILTON-BURR DUEL

FIORELLO LA GUARDIA

CROTON RESERVOIR

MRS. MURRAY ENTERTAINS

EAST RIVER

TRAMCAR

SEVENTH REGIMENT
PARADE

TOM THUMB

PETER STUYVESANT

THE HALF MOON

THE MONITOR

WASHINGTON'S INAUGURATION

MORSE CODE

AL SMITH

CAPTAIN KIDD

WASHINGTON ROEBLING

DUTCH
WINDMILL

ELLIS ISLAND

BRITISH MAN O' WAR

PETER MINUIT

JOHN PETER ZENGER

JENNIE JEROME

SOME HELPFUL HINTS FOR VISITING PARENTS—AND FOR YOU, TOO

WE almost called this book "After the Empire State Building, What?" So many New York visitors ask: "What else is there to see?" after they and their children have taken in the conventional sights—the enormous building mentioned above, Rockefeller Center, the Museum of Natural History, the Planetarium and the Statue of Liberty. You will certainly find all these on our maps, but we have added other places we feel will interest children and spark them to explore the town more thoroughly on their own.

New York is so vast it often overawes the visitor into a state of immobility, and many a native New Yorker knows only a small segment of it—from home to school or office and back home again. By carving the big town into manageable chunks on our maps, we hope we have brought it down to an explorable scale.

We have pointed arrows to sections of the town we think will amuse children. We have skipped parts that won't. After exploring, you may say "Why, we spent a wonderful afternoon on a street they left out!" Nothing would please us more; it will mean we have broken through the occupational lethargy of sight-seeing, tempted you off the obvious tracks, and sent you exploring on your own.

One hazard this book—and other guide books—can't avoid: some of the buildings we have shown may be torn down by the time you read this, some of the shops relocated. But we can promise you that whatever is built in their places will be worth investigating. New York always grows more magnificent. As for other guide books, Kate Simon's "New York Places and Pleasures, An Uncommon Guide" is one of the best and available in good book stores. At stationery stores and newsstands you can buy the "Little Red Book, The Complete Street Guide to New York."

And now, a few practical suggestions that may save you time, trouble, and money before and during your visit to New York.

BEFORE YOU COME TO TOWN

- Your own branch of the AAA has listings of New York hotels, noting which ones welcome children, and giving price scales. Esso stations have lists, too.

- If you want to see a TV show, write well ahead for tickets (especially if it's Perry Como-or-nobody for your family) to CBS, 485 Madison Avenue; NBC, Rockefeller Center; ABC, 39 West 66th Street.

- Bring comfortable shoes because you will want to walk a great deal; and taxis, though not expensive, are sometimes hard to find.

- Comfortable clothes are in order, also. New Yorkers aren't strong for hats, but if *you* are, wear one. Even in summer, some New York restaurants insist on a coat and tie for men.

Your son will want a jacket (tuck a tie in the pocket) for the air-conditioned places just as your daughter will need a light sweater.

- Bring your watch; clocks are hard to spot.

- Bring Travelers Checks. Your own hotel will cash your personal check on the strength of your driver's license, but shops sometimes balk at this. (Keep lots of dimes in your pockets—for telephones and toilets).

IN NEW YORK

- The policemen are your best allies. They will tell you where it is and how to get there. Should you and your children lose each other, they will lend bus fare to get back to the hotel.

(Please turn the page)

- The newspapers are essential to planning a rewarding visit. On Wednesdays *The New York Times* runs a feature listing events of interest to children; on Thursdays and Sundays check the *Herald-Tribune;* on Fridays and Saturdays the *World-Telegram & Sun;* on Saturdays the *Post*. And the *Daily News* is helpful if you call for information. *The New Yorker* magazine and *Cue* have children's sections and listings of the movies around town also. (In addition, *Cue* has a helpful listing of restaurants.)

- Radio stations WNYC, WQXR and WPAT make frequent announcements of current New York events, as well as hourly weather reports.

- The telephone is always handy, and don't be shy about using it. New Yorkers live by the telephone and are thoroughly conditioned to answering telephoned questions.

- Doormen, waiters, waitresses, taxi drivers are almost always people who are proud of their city and like to talk about it. They are much better targets for your questions than a passerby—who is likely to be another visitor.

- Shopping in New York is much like shopping anywhere. The prices in the big stores are about the same as in your best stores at home (comparison shoppers help keep prices uniform). Steer clear of stores announcing they are "Selling Out"; they are usually fake sales of shoddy merchandise.

- Eating in New York is a twenty-four-hour-a-day affair. This is a break for you because you will find you and your children will stay happy and unweary longer if you stop often for a snack. Avoid the lunch crowds that pour into almost every restaurant between twelve and two, and instead plan on brief eating breaks at eleven, two-thirty, and four-thirty.

- Conventions or other meetings may be the reason for your trip to New York. Don't despair; you won't have to leave the children tucked away in a hotel room. There are two delightful services especially designed to meet this situation. *Part-Time Child Care, Inc.,* 19 East 69th Street, the most highly recommended of the baby-sitting agencies will supply you with a trained baby-sitter to watch over and amuse the younger members of your safari. Give them, if possible, several days notice, especially weekends. *Gulliver's Trails,* 25 Central Park West, is a well-run organization that will pick up your children at your hotel and take them on imaginative tours of the city, chaperoned by trained teachers and camp counselors.

- For the foreign-born, whose curiosity is stronger than their English, *Gray Line Tours,* 245 West 50th Street, has busses equipped with individual headsets that deliver running commentary in French, German, Spanish and Japanese as they tour around the island.

- A final word to explorers: be sure to check first to avoid disappointments. Most museums are closed Mondays and national holidays, for instance, so make a call in advance to be sure. For events in any park, check with the New York Department of Parks. And lastly, we strongly urge you to drop in to the New York Convention and Visitors Bureau, 90 East 42nd Street (near Grand Central). They have their own "Visitor's Guide and Map of New York" that is small in size but big in information. They will supply other booklets, all free, and are very kind about answering questions about anything in and around New York.

HAVE A WONDERFUL TIME!

INDEX

BROOKLYN BRIDGE, 31, 35
Connects Park Row in Manhattan with High Street, Brooklyn. Pedestrians allowed. Walk across for a fine view.

BROOKLYN CHILDREN'S MUSEUM, 35
Brooklyn Avenue and Park Place, Brooklyn
BMT, IRT Lexington or 7th Avenue subways. Open weekdays 10 a.m. to 5 p.m.; Sundays and holidays 1 to 5 p.m.

BROOKLYN HEIGHTS, 31

BROOKLYN OPERA COMPANY, 38
Academy of Music, 30 Lafayette Avenue, Brooklyn
"Hansel and Gretel" is performed during Christmas season. For this and other seasonal events, watch newspapers, *The New Yorker* and *Cue*.

BROOKS BROTHERS, 12
346 Madison Avenue, 44th Street
Everything for men from eight to eighty, from bow ties to nightcaps.

BRYANT PARK, 9, 13
Behind Public Library, 40th to 42nd Streets, off Fifth Avenue
Concerts of classical music piped in during summer from noon to 2 p.m.

BUDDHIST CHURCH, 30, 32
333 Riverside Drive, 105th Street
Look for statue of Buddhist saint.

BUTTON SHOP—OLD BUTTONS, INC., 23
510 Madison Avenue, near 54th Street
Bright buttons, old buttons, pretty buttons to change a dress, to make into earrings or cuff links for presents.

CAFE DE LA PAIX, 10
50 Central Park South, St. Moritz Hotel

CANAL STREET, 25

CANADA HOUSE, 11
680 Fifth Avenue, 53rd Street
Shields of the 10 provinces are outside the entrance.

CARNEGIE HALL, 10
57th Street at Seventh Avenue

CAROUSEL (FRIEDSAM MEMORIAL), 17
Central Park, near Heckscher Playground
Open all year, weather permitting.

CARTIER'S, INC., 11
Fifth Avenue at 52nd Street
Don't rush by the shadow boxes here. You may see a diamond resting like a butterfly on a paper flower.

CATHEDRAL OF ST. JOHN THE DIVINE, P.E., 32
Amsterdam Avenue and 112th Street
Not yet completed, it will be the largest Gothic cathedral in the world.

CEDAR HILL, 15
Central Park, off Fifth Avenue at 79th Street

CENTRAL PARK ZOO, 14, 17
Central Park, behind Arsenal off Fifth Avenue at 64th Street
Open all year 8 a.m. to 8 p.m. (closes slightly earlier in winter). Cafeteria open all year.

CHASE MANHATTAN BANK, 29
1 Chase Manhattan Plaza
Breathtaking view of harbor from its observation deck, 58th floor. Tours 9:30 and 10 a.m.; 3 and 3:30 p.m. Call to confirm tour reservations.

CHERRY BLOSSOM TIME, 39
Brooklyn Botanic Gardens
Annual house, garden and private gallery tours, as well as a wealth of cherry blossoms on Cherry Walk.

CHILDREN'S THEATERS—CRICKET THEATER, 26
162 Second Avenue, 10th Street
Children's plays on Saturdays. Check children's sections in newspapers, *The New Yorker* and *Cue* for other plays of interest to children in other theaters.

CHILDREN'S ZOO, 17
Central Park, off Fifth Avenue between 65th and 66th Streets (entrance in front of Arsenal, 64th Street)
Donated by Mr. and Mrs. Herbert H. Leh-

man. It has Noah's Ark, animals to hold. Adults must be chaperoned by children every day except Monday.

CHINATOWN, 25, 28, 38
Mott, Pell, Doyer and Mulberry Streets
Paper dragons come out of hiding for Chinese New Year in February. Watch newspaper for dates.

CHOCK FULL O' NUTS, 11
532 Madison Avenue, 54th Street
Fresh orange drink, sandwiches and doughnuts "untouched by human hands." Shops all over town.

CHRISTMAS EVENTS

CHRISTMAS MOVIES, 38
Junior Museum, Metropolitan Museum, Fifth Avenue at 82nd Street

DO-IT-YOURSELF CHRISTMAS CARDS, 38
Brandon Memorabilia, 215 East 59th Street
Old fashioned greeting cards as well as the materials to make your own.

"HANSEL AND GRETEL," 38
Performed during Christmas holidays by the Brooklyn Opera Company, Brooklyn Academy of Music. For this and other seasonal operas, plays and marionette shows, consult the children's sections in newspapers, *The New Yorker* and *Cue*.

NEW YORK CITY BALLET, 36, 38
City Center, 131 West 55th Street
Tchaikovsky's "Nutcracker Suite" danced here during Christmas season.

PLANETARIUM, 38
Hayden Planetarium shows Christmas skies as they appeared at the time of the Nativity. See newspaper for times, dates.

ROCKEFELLER CENTER TREE AND CAROLEERS, 38
Rockefeller Plaza, Fifth Avenue between 49th and 50th Streets
Christmas tree goes up first Tuesday in December. For dates and times of concerts by caroleers, see newspapers.

ST. THOMAS' CHURCH, P.E., 38
Fifth Avenue and 53rd Street
On Sunday evening preceding Christmas Eve, choral and manger service by candlelight. See newspaper for Christmas services in other churches.

SAKS FIFTH AVENUE PIPE ORGAN, 38
Fifth Avenue at 49th Street
Built anew each Christmas, it plays Christmas carols for shoppers.

SEAGRAM BUILDING CHRISTMAS TREES, 36, 38
Park Avenue, 52 to 53rd Streets
Amber lights on trees placed in the pools glow against the amber building.

WALLACHS BROUGHAM, 38
It goes up and down Fifth Avenue during the Christmas season filled with Christmas-wrapped packages.

CHRISTMAS MOVIES
see "Christmas Events"

CITY HALL, 25, 28
Broadway and Park Row
Seat of New York City government since 1812. It is a fine example of Federal architecture.

CIRCUS—RINGLING BROTHERS BARNUM AND BAILEY, 39
Madison Square Garden, Eighth Avenue and 49th Street
See newspaper for times, dates.

CLEOPATRA'S NEEDLE (OBELISK), 19
Central Park off East Drive, near 81st Street and Metropolitan Museum
This obelisk dates from 1500 B.C. It was presented by the Khedive of Egypt in 1869. It took 96 days to haul it from the harbor to the Park.

THE CLERMONT, 44
Robert Fulton invented this steamboat which was launched August 7, 1807.

THE CLOISTERS, 30, 32
Fort Tryon Park, IND "A" train to 190th Street
Open 10 a.m. to 5 p.m. except Mondays; 1 to 5 p.m. Sundays; to 6 p.m. in summer.

ROSE FESTIVAL, 40
Bronx Botanical Gardens, early in June
Roses in demonstrations, in lectures, in the gardens. Lovely to look at (and smell) before and after specific date.

FINCHLEY, INC., 6
564 Fifth Avenue, near 46th Street

FIRE-FIGHTING MUSEUM OF THE HOME INSURANCE COMPANY, 29
59 Maiden Lane
Temporarily closed due to construction of 44 story skyscraper, The Home's museum is one of the largest fire-fighting collections in the world. Scheduled to reopen early 1966.

FIREWORKS, 40
Macy's display: Riverside Drive, June 27th.
Coney Island: July 4th; every Tuesday night in summer. See newspaper.

FIRST PRESBYTERIAN CHURCH, 24, 26
Fifth Avenue at 12th Street

FLATIRON BUILDING, 13
Broadway at 23rd Street
This was the first New York steel-built skyscraper.

FLOWER MARKET, 5, 30, 33
between West 27th and West 28th Streets on Sixth Avenue
Most establishments here are wholesale, but will sell you leftovers at bargain prices. Open from 6:30 to 10 a.m.

FLOWER SHOW, 36, 39
Coliseum, 59th Street and Broadway
March; see newspapers for dates.

FOLEY SQUARE — NEW YORK CITY AND NEW YORK STATE COURT BUILDINGS, FEDERAL BUILDINGS, 25, 28
Foley Square, City Hall Park
The government buildings of city, state and nation surround this square.

FOREST HILLS — WEST SIDE TENNIS CLUB, 37, 41
Forest Hills, Queens
National championship tennis matches held here in late August or early September. See newspaper for dates.

FORT TRYON PARK, 32
Broadway and Nagle Avenue
The Cloisters museum is here.

FRAUNCES TAVERN RESTAURANT, 29
Broad and Pearl Streets
Oldest building in the city, it was built in 1719. Washington said farewell to his officers here. Now it's a good restaurant.

FREEDOMLAND, 34, 37, 40
Baychester and Barrow Avenues, The Bronx
IRT Dyre Avenue line to Gun Hill Road station; IRT Lexington Avenue, No. 6, to Pelham Park station; shuttle bus to park from both stations. Open 10 a.m. to 11 p.m. every day from Memorial Day to Labor Day. Open Saturdays and Sundays until late October.

FRICK MUSEUM, 16
Fifth Avenue at 70th Street
Open 10 a.m. to 5 p.m. Tuesday through Saturday, 1 to 5 p.m. Sundays and holidays. Closed Mondays and the month of August. This is a magnificent collection of 14th to 19th century European art in a magnificent house. Children under 11 not allowed; those under 16 must be accompanied by adults.

FRUIT BOATS—NEW JERSEY, 33
Boats bring in some of the 21 billion pounds of meats, 4½ billion pounds of fruit and vegetables (*and* the 155 million dozen eggs) New Yorkers eat each year.

FULTON FISH MARKET, 25, 29
Fulton Street at East River
This is a place for early morning exploration since the market is left to the gulls by 8 a.m. Breakfast with drivers and merchants at Sloppy Louie's, 92 South Street. Plan lunch or dinner at Sweet's, at the corner of Fulton and South Streets.

GARMENT DISTRICT, 13
Seventh Avenue in the 30's
One of the most crowded sections of New York in which you'll bump into next year's dresses, coats and suits and brush by a truck of mink.

GAY STREET, 24, 26
off Christopher Street
Shortest street in the city with some of the oldest houses in Greenwich Village.

GEORG JENSEN, INC., 11
667 Fifth Avenue at 53rd Street
Danish silver, linens, jewelry, toys.

GEORGE WASHINGTON BRIDGE, 31, 34
Manhattan entrance: 175th Street and West Side Highway; New Jersey exit: Fort Lee
Pedestrians allowed. It is a long walk across, but it provides a beautiful view of Manhattan and the Hudson.

GIMBEL'S, 30, 33
Sixth Avenue and 33rd Street
In addition to being a complete department store, Gimbel's has one of the best coin and stamp collections in New York.

GLASS BLOWER — ARTISTIC GLASS SPINNER, 33
768 Eighth Avenue, 47th Street
Bring a sketch of your pet and skilled Japanese glass blowers will spin him in glass before your eyes.

GOVERNOR'S ISLAND (FORT JAY)
New York Harbor; ferry from Battery Park.
Headquarters of U. S. First Army. Public parade at retreat Wednesdays at 5 p.m. May through November there are tours of the entire island for children 11 and up. For either parade or tour, write for a pass, Post Information Office, Fort Jay. The island can be visited freely; children must be accompanied.

GRACIE MANSION, 30, 32
Carl Schurz Park at 89th Street (at East River)
This is the official home of New York mayors. The fireboat stationed in the East River by the mansion may be visited.

GRAMERCY PARK, 24
20th to 21st Streets between Third Avenue and Park Avenue South

GRAND CENTRAL STATION, 9, 21, 23
East 42nd Street from Vanderbilt to Lexington Avenues
Restaurants, bookshops, newsreel theater, restrooms (boys may shower here), and a whispering gallery — for two players. Stand outside the Oyster Bar between Main and Lower levels and place your partner diagonally across the passageway. You can hear each other's gentlest words, but nobody else can.

GRAND TICINO RESTAURANT, 27
228 Thompson Street
One of the good Italian restaurants that dot Greenwich Village.

GRANT'S TOMB, 30, 32
Riverside Drive at 123rd Street
Open 9 a.m. to 5 p.m. On the slope below the tomb is a stone urn with the inscription "Erected to the memory of an amiable child" and dated July 15, 1797. St. Clair Pollack was the amiable little boy so kindly remembered.

GRAY LINE TOURS, 49
245 West 50th Street
New York tours by bus with comments in French, German, Spanish and Japanese in addition to English.

THE GREAT LAWN, 19
Central Park, 81st to 85th Streets

GREENWICH HOUSE POTTERY, 27
16 Jones Street
Exhibit cycle of pottery from clay to finished piece on show daily October to June.

GRIPSOLM RESTAURANT, 10
324 East 57th Street, near First Avenue
Smorgasbord. Don't take everything you like from the deliciously laden table at once. You can go back again and again and again.

GROCERIES AND BAKERIES, 23
For an apple to eat while you're walking,

stop at Savoy Market, 50th Street and Second Avenue. For a piece of French pastry, look in on Ross Pastry Shop, 922 Second Avenue.

GUGGENHEIM MUSEUM (SOLOMON R.), 18
Fifth Avenue at 88th Street
Open Tuesday through Saturday 10 a.m. to 6 p.m. (to 9 p.m. Wednesdays); Sundays 12 N. to 6 p.m. Closed Mondays. Modern paintings and sculpture exhibited in a modern setting designed by Frank Lloyd Wright who prophesied future "cities of glass and steel where the sirens of the fire engines will never be heard."

GULLIVER'S TRAILS, 49
25 Central Park West

HALE, NATHAN, 45
Captured by the British during the Revolutionary War, Hale was hanged as a spy September 22, 1776. He said, "I only regret that I have but one life to lose for my country."

HALF MOON, 42, 45
Henry Hudson sailed up the Hudson River in the Half Moon.

HALL OF FAME FOR GREAT AMERICANS, 32
181st Street and University Avenue
IRT Lexington Avenue subway. Open 9 a.m. until sundown. This open colonnade displays busts of famous citizens of the United States.

HALLOWEEN IN THE VILLAGE, 37, 41

HAMILTON, ALEXANDER, 25

HAMILTON AND BURR DUEL, 45
On July 11, 1804, at Weehawken, New Jersey, a duel resolved a bitter political feud between Alexander Hamilton and Aaron Burr. Hamilton did not fire his pistol; Burr did. Hamilton was wounded and later died in Greenwich Village.

"HANGING TREE," 24

"HANSEL AND GRETEL"
see "Christmas Events"

HANUKKAH, 38
The Jewish Feast of Dedication, or Festival of Lights, is celebrated in December in homes and synagogues. Check newspaper for big celebration in Madison Square Garden.

HAYDEN PLANETARIUM—AMERICAN MUSEUM OF NATURAL HISTORY, 15, 19, 46
Central Park West at 81st Street
Shows Monday through Friday at 2, 2:30, and 8:30 p.m. (no 8:30 performance Mondays); 11 a.m., 1, 2, 3, 4, 5, and 8:30 p.m. Saturdays, Sundays and holidays (no 11 a.m. performance on Sundays and holidays). Besides the regular performances in the 75 foot planetarium dome, displays of astronomical instruments, models, photographs and materials are shown.

HELIPORT, 33
East River Pier 6, foot of Wall Street
Nine minutes (in the air) of sightseeing above the city. Three passengers can ride at a time in a helicopter; two small (under 12) children count as one person. Call for flight times.

HERALD SQUARE, 13

HICKS, H. & SON, INC., 12
16 East 49th Street, between Fifth and Madison Avenues
Oldest soda fountain in New York, first established 1863 at the tip of the Island.

HOLLAND TUNNEL, 35
New York entrance: Canal Street; New Jersey exit: Jersey City

HOME INSURANCE COMPANY, 29
59 Maiden Lane

HORSE SHOW, 41
Madison Square Garden, Eighth Avenue and 49th Street
International Horse Show is held the first week of November every year. Check newspaper for exact dates and times.

HORSEBACK RIDING, 17
Horses to rent at Claremont Riding Academy, *175 West 89th Street.*

HUDSON, HENRY, 42

HUDSON BOAT TRIPS, 40
Day Line, Pier 81, foot of West 41st Street; March through October 9:30, 10:30 a.m., 1, 2 p.m.

ICECAPADES, 41
Madison Square Garden
The new Icecapades show plays New York in late August or early September. See newspaper for exact dates.

ICE SKATING, 17, 37, 41
Rockefeller Plaza, Rockefeller Center, off Fifth Avenue between 49th and 50th Streets.
Wollman Memorial Rink, Central Park off East Drive about 62nd Street.

INDOOR POLO, 39
Squadron A Armory, Madison Avenue at 94th Street. Check newspaper for dates.

INTERNATIONAL AIRPORT (NEW YORK INTERNATIONAL AIRPORT, NOW CALLED "JOHN F. KENNEDY" AIRPORT), 31, 35
Bus from East Side Airlines Terminal takes you directly to the airport. Ride "flightseer" to observation deck. There is also an animal airport there.

INWOOD HILL PARK, 30, 32, 44
Payson Avenue and Dyckman Street
IND "A" train subway to 207th Street. This area was much the same when Indians lived here. It is a great spot for picnicking.

JAPANESE FOLKCRAFT, 27
167 West 4th Street

JENNIE JEROME, 45
Winston Churchill's mother was born at 426 Henry Street, Brooklyn, in 1854.

JEWISH MUSEUM, 18
Fifth Avenue and 92nd Street
Open Monday through Thursday 1 to 5 p.m.; Sundays 11 a.m. to 6 p.m. Closed Fridays, Saturdays and the month of July. Jewish ceremonial objects from many centuries and countries as well as from contemporary Israel.

JOHN W. BROWN TRAINING SHIP, 33
East River Pier 73, 24th Street
Boys are trained here for the Merchant Marine. Maritime Service Ship may be visited during school hours on school days.

JONES BEACH STATE PARK, 35, 37, 40
South Shore, Long Island
This park has five miles of beach, the Marine Stadium, play fields, restaurants, huge parking lots, snack bars and locker rooms, all kept in top-notch condition. It is open all year.

JON'S SCANDINAVIAN SHOP, 27
179 West 4th Street, near Sixth Avenue

JUMBLE SHOP RESTAURANT, 26
28 West 8th Street, corner of MacDougal Street
Watch your steak broil on the open hearth. The buffalo nickel was designed here by James Earl Frazer when the building was a studio.

JUMEL MANSION, 32
Edgecombe Avenue and 161st Street
8th Avenue subway to 163rd Street station. A colonial cannon stands in front of this handsome colonial mansion beautifully restored to appear as it did when it was George Washington's headquarters during the American Revolution.

JUNIOR MUSEUM — METROPOLITAN MUSEUM, 15, 19
Fifth Avenue and 82nd Street
Special exhibits of interest to young people. See newspaper for Christmas movie schedule.

JUNIOR OLYMPICS, 41
Track, field, boxing, wrestling, and bicycle racing contests for young people in city parks. For park and dates, call Department of Parks in September.

CAPTAIN KIDD, 45
He lived at 119-121 Pearl Street about 1691. English merchants commissioned him to rid the seas of pirates, but he was later hanged as a pirate himself.

KNICKERBOCKERS, 44
This was the first organized baseball team in New York.

KLEIN'S ON THE SQUARE, 26
6 Union Square
This self-service department store has amazing bargains for the stout of heart and limb.

KRESS, 13
444 Fifth Avenue, 39th Street
Fifth Avenue version of a 10¢ store—it sells diamonds.

LA GUARDIA AIRPORT, 34
Jackson Heights, Queens
Busses from East Side Airlines Terminal, 37th Street and First Avenue.

LA GUARDIA, FIORELLO, 45
LaGuardia was mayor of New York from 1934 to 1945. He was called "The Little Flower," but fought city corruption in a most un-flower-like way! He also chased fire engines and read comics to city children over radio during a newspaper strike. He renamed Sixth Avenue "Avenue of the Americas."

THE LAKE, 16
Central Park, West Drive near 72nd Street
Fishing in season, rowboats for hire. Loeb Memorial Boathouse and a cafeteria are here.

LEVER BUILDING, 23
390 Park Avenue, 54th Street
An exhibit of children's art work sponsored by the Board of Education is shown on the first floor of this beautiful building in spring. The building is open weekdays 9 a.m. to 5 p.m.; Saturdays, Sundays and holidays 1 to 5 p.m.

LEWISOHN STADIUM, 32, 40
138th Street and Amsterdam Avenue
Fifth Avenue bus No. 3; IRT Broadway subway. From the last week in June to the end of August summer concerts are held under the stars. See newspapers for times, performers and dates.

LIBRARY—NEW YORK PUBLIC LIBRARY, 9, 13, 36
42nd Street and Fifth Avenue
The famous proud library lions guard more than four million books at the main branch of New York's vast public library. The Children's Room has a great collection of picture books and other books for young people; there are story-telling hours (call the library and ask for "Children's Room" to find out exactly when and where). Special exhibits often on view.

DONNELL LIBRARY, 11
20 West 53rd Street
This branch of the library houses the Nathan Straus Children's Collections.

LINCOLN, ABRAHAM, 43

LINCOLN CENTER FOR THE PERFORMING ARTS, 17, 41
Broadway at 65th Street
Lincoln Center will eventually contain, all in one area: Philharmonic Hall, the Metropolitan Opera House, the New York State Theater, Vivian Beaumont Theater, Julliard School of Music, and the Library and Museum of the Performing Arts.

LINCOLN TUNNEL, 35
New York entrance: 34th Street; New Jersey exit: Union City

LIONEL TRAIN EXHIBIT, 30, 33
15 East 26th Street, off Madison Avenue

LITTLE CARNEGIE THEATER, 10
146 West 57th Street
Foreign films and movies of interest to children. Watch newspapers for listings.

"LITTLE CHURCH AROUND THE CORNER"—Church of the Transfiguration, P.E., 13
1 East 29th Street
This lovely church acquired its name in 1870 when the minister of a fashionable church refused burial to an actor and suggested to a friend that he try "the little church around the corner."

LITTLE RED LIGHTHOUSE — Jeffrey's Hook Lighthouse, 34
Fort Washington Avenue and 178th Street
Picnic under the George Washington Bridge along the Hudson by a lighthouse (now closed).

LORD & TAYLOR, 9, 13, 36
Fifth Avenue at 38th Street
An old New York name in stores with the newest clothes, many imported.

LUCHOW'S RESTAURANT, 26
110 East 14th Street
Established in 1882; serves fine German dishes in an Old World setting.

McARTHUR'S SHELL SHOP, 30, 33
590 Third Avenue, near 39th Street

MacDOUGAL STREET, 24, 26, 27

MACY'S, 13, 37, 41
Herald Square (Broadway) to Seventh Avenue, between 34th and 35th Streets.

MADISON SQUARE GARDEN, 22
Eighth Avenue at 49th Street
This is the largest indoor stadium in the city for sports, public events and entertainment. It will move in 1964 or 1965 to new quarters built over Penn Station.

MAGIC CENTER, 22
739 Eighth Avenue, near 45th Street
Magicians' equipment for sale and magic tricks taught at the Institute of Magic.

MAIDEN LANE, 25, 29, 42
Off Broadway downtown
Don't miss clock in the sidewalk. Maiden Lane is insurance center.

THE MALL, 14, 16
Central Park, East Drive between 69th and 72nd Streets

MANUFACTURERS HANOVER TRUST, 12
510 Fifth Avenue, 43rd Street
See the huge vault in plain view of front windows.

MARINE MUSEUM OF THE SEAMEN'S CHURCH INSTITUTE OF NEW YORK, 29
25 South Street
Seaworthy collection of ship models. There is a lighthouse on the roof to visit.

MARIONETTES, 19
Swedish Schoolhouse, Central Park, West Drive near 79th Street
A traveling marionette show is kept in the Swedish Schoolhouse. In summer, shows are given in city parks and playgrounds. Call the Department of Parks for information.

MAYPOLE DANCING, 39
Danced by various schools in various sections of the city. Check when and where by calling the Department of Parks early in May.

METROPOLITAN MUSEUM OF ART, 15, 19
Fifth Avenue at 82nd Street
For a brief rest from the glory that is displayed here, find the cafeteria by the indoor pool. Museum open Tuesday through Saturday, 10 a.m. to 5 p.m.; Sundays and holidays 1 to 5 p.m. Closed Mondays.

MILLAY HOUSE, 24, 27
75½ Bedford Street
This is the narrowest house (10 feet) in Manhattan.

MINUIT, PETER, 45
In 1626 as governor of New Netherlands, he bought Manhattan Island from Indians for beads worth about $24.

MODEL BOAT REGATTA, 40
Conservatory Pond, Central Park
Anyone under 18 may enter a sailboat in the annual regatta which is held in June.

MONEYS OF THE WORLD, 22
Exhibit of moneys from all over the world in Chase Manhattan's bank at Rockefeller Plaza at 49th Street is open 10 a.m. to 5 p.m. weekdays only.

THE MONITOR, 45
John Ericsson built the first "iron ship" on West Street. It was launched January 30, 1862, and fought the Confederate ironclad Merrimac in a fierce battle at Hampton Roads, Virginia.

MORSE CODE, 45
Samuel F. B. Morse was a professor at New York University from 1832 to 1837. In 1843 Congress voted him $30,000 to build telegraph line on which on May 24, 1844, he sent the first telegraph message: "What hath God wrought."

MORSE, SAMUEL F. B.
see "Morse Code"

MURRAY, MRS. ROBERT, 45
Mrs. Murray, wife of a Quaker merchant, delayed British General Howe with lunch long enough for General Rufus Putnam and his men to escape up the island during the Revolution. Look for plaque in honor of Mrs. Murray in the Park Avenue mall at 37th Street.

MUSEUM OF THE AMERICAN INDIAN, HEYE FOUNDATION, 32
Broadway and 155th Street
Open Tuesday through Sunday 1 to 5 p.m. Closed Mondays, holidays and the months of July and August. Collections of the art and culture of the Indians of the Americas are on display here.

MUSEUM OF THE CITY OF NEW YORK, 15, 18, 25
Fifth Avenue at 103rd Street
Open Tuesday through Saturday 10 a.m. to 5 p.m. Sundays and holidays 1 to 5 p.m. Closed Mondays. Dolls, toys, dioramas, ship models, fire engines and New Yorkiana are on display here. Children's movies, walking tours of the city and lectures are also given. Call museum for information.

MUSEUM OF CONTEMPORARY CRAFTS, 11
29 West 53rd Street
Open 12 N. to 6 p.m. daily; 2 to 6 p.m. Sundays. This museum shows modern furniture, fabrics and decorations of the United States and occasionally exhibits from other countries.

MUSEUM OF MODERN ART, 11
11 West 53rd Street
Open 11 a.m. to 6 p.m. (10 p.m. Thursdays); Sundays 1 to 7 p.m. Exhibits are shown here of contemporary painting, sculpture, architecture, industrial design and photography. Old movies are also shown; check newspaper for schedules. There is a cafeteria by the garden open all year. Admission is $1.00 for adults; 25¢ for children under 12.

MUSEUM OF NATURAL HISTORY, 15, 19, 46
Central Park West at 81st Street
Open Monday through Saturday 10 a.m. to 5 p.m.; Sundays and holidays 1 to 5 p.m. This is one of the greatest collections of plant and animal life in the world. There are jewels, masks, and carvings of all cultures of the globe, too. Recordings with earphones available.

MUSEUM OF PRIMITIVE ART, 11
15 West 54th Street
Open 2 to 5 p.m. weekdays; 1 to 5 p.m. Sundays. Closed Mondays. This is a permanent collection from Oceania, Africa and the Americas.

NATIONAL BROADCASTING COMPANY, 47
30 Rockefeller Plaza

NEDICK'S, 22
Corner of Broadway and 50th Street, and all over the city
Stop for a quick orange drink.

NEW YORK BOTANICAL GARDEN, 31, 34
Bronx Park, The Bronx
IRT Lexington Avenue or IND subway. Two hundred and thirty acres of virgin forest, lawns, and 12,000 different plants can be seen here. There are also conservatories, seasonal flower displays. See newspaper for dates.

NEW YORK CITY BALLET, 36
City Center, 131 West 55th Street
see "Christmas Events"

NEW YORK CITY CENTER, 22, 36
131 West 55th Street, west of Sixth Avenue

NEW YORK CONVENTION AND VISITORS' BUREAU, 49
90 East 42nd Street

NEW YORK DAILY NEWS, 13, 48
see "The Daily News"

NEW YORK DOLL HOSPITAL, 33
1021 Third Avenue, near 60th Street
Dolls and toys repaired. Ailing dolls are mailed from as far away as New Delhi.

THE NEW YORK EXCHANGE FOR WOMAN'S WORK, 11
541 Madison Avenue, near 54th Street
Stuffed animals, crayon baskets, and patchwork quilts for dolls, all handmade, are for sale upstairs. Downstairs is a good restaurant.

NEW YORK HERALD TRIBUNE, 48
230 West 41st Street

NEW YORK HISTORICAL SOCIETY, 15, 19, 25
170 Central Park West, near 76th Street
Open weekdays and Sundays 1 to 5 p.m.; Saturdays 10 a.m. to 5 p.m. Closed Mondays, holidays and the month of August. Magnificent marine collection is housed here as well as old time carriages, sleds, fire fighting equipment, toys and dolls, military and naval history artifacts.

NEW YORK POST, 48
75 West Street

NEW YORK STOCK EXCHANGE, 25, 29
Wall and Broad Streets
Visitors can watch operations of the nation's largest securities market from the balcony Monday through Friday 10 a.m. to 3 p.m.

NEW YORK TIMES, 48
229 West 43rd Street

NEW YORK TIMES TOWER, 22
Times Square at 42nd Street
Out-of-town newspaper stand at 43rd Street side. Official Visitor Information Center open from 9 a.m. to 6 p.m. daily.

NEW YORK WORLD TELEGRAM AND SUN, 48
125 Barclay Street

NEW YORK UNIVERSITY, 27
Washington Square, Manhattan, and University Heights, The Bronx
Buildings and departments of NYU are scattered all around New York. It is the world's largest private university with over 43,000 students in its various colleges.

NEW YORK YACHT CLUB, 6
37 West 44th Street, off Fifth Avenue

THE NEW YORKER MAGAZINE, 48

NORTHERN DISPENSARY, 27
Waverly Place and Christopher Street
One of the oldest health clinics in the city (certainly the oddest shaped); Poe had a cold treated here.

OLD MERCHANT'S HOUSE, 27
29 East 4th Street
Open Tuesday through Saturday 11 a.m. to 5 p.m.; Sundays and holidays 1 to 5 p.m. Here are preserved clothes and furniture just as they were in the 1800's. Find the hidden staircase (rumored used by smugglers).

OLIVETTI, 9, 12
584 Fifth Avenue, near 47th Street
Typewriters. The one on the street you may try out.

ORCHARD STREET, 25

OUTDOOR ART SHOW, 27, 39, 41
Washington Square
In spring and fall artists show work around the square. Watch newspapers for dates.

PARADES
(on Fifth Avenue unless otherwise noted)

ARMED FORCES DAY, May 1

COLUMBUS DAY, October 12

EASTER PARADE, Easter Sunday, 39
More a crowd than a parade, as models as well as Easter worshipers from St. Patrick's, St. Thomas' and other churches walk up Fifth Avenue.

FEDERATION OF HELLENIC (GREEK) AMERICAN SOCIETIES, first week in April

ST. PAUL'S CHAPEL, P.E., 29, 43
Broadway and Fulton Streets
The oldest public building on the Island turns its back on Broadway. Each column contains a different kind of English tree. George Washington worshipped here.

ST. THOMAS' CHURCH, P.E., 8
Fifth Avenue and 53rd Street
Beautiful windows and reredos. Also see "Christmas Events."

SAITO RESTAURANT, 11
70 West 55th Street
Japanese food that you can eat sitting on the floor or at western-height tables.

SAKS FIFTH AVENUE, 8
Fifth Avenue and 49th Street

SAKS FIFTH AVENUE PIPE ORGAN
see "Christmas Events"

SALMAGUNDI CLUB, 26
47 Fifth Avenue
See gaslights on either side of the entrance.

SARDI BUS, 23
from Sardi's East, 123 East 54th Street, to Sardi's, 234 West 44th Street
This bus was imported from London and is the only double-decker bus in the United States. It runs for the convenience of Sardi's (famous theatrical restaurant) customers.

G. SCHIRMER, INC., 12
4 East 49th Street, off Fifth Avenue
Here you will find all musical instruments, music and records from Bach to Basie.

SCHRAFFT'S, 12
556 Fifth Avenue, near 46th Street
One of the many Schrafft's in New York, it has four floors of dining rooms and almost every sort of meal. Schraffts are neighborly, friendly restaurants with wonderful desserts and candies.

F. A. O. SCHWARZ, 8, 10, 38
745 Fifth Avenue, 58th Street
The best-known toy shop in the world; it has books, too.

SCRIBNER'S, 8
597 Fifth Avenue, near 48th Street

SEAGRAM BUILDING, 23, 36
375 Park Avenue, 52nd Street
Look for the pool in front. In summer it's a cool place to rest; at Christmas there are lighted trees. See "Christmas Events."

SECONDHAND BOOKSTORES, 26
Astor Place to 14th Street on Fourth Avenue
Street stalls and bookshops for treasure-hunting books. Schultes, 80 Fourth Avenue, and O'Malley's, 377 Park Avenue South, are two of the best.

SEVENTH REGIMENT, 45
645 Park Avenue
New York's own regiment, and its oldest.

SHAKESPEARE FESTIVAL, 19, 40
Central Park by Belvedere Tower, off 79th Street
Nightly except Mondays in July and August free Shakespeare plays are presented by the Shakespeare Festival of New York. See newspapers for plays and dates.

SHAKESPEARE GARDEN, 15, 19
Central Park, West Drive near 79th Street
Besides the sundial, this garden has all the plants and shrubs mentioned in Shakespeare's writings. Find "Rosemary—that's for remembrance."

SHELL SHOP – McARTHUR'S SHELL SHOP, 30, 33
590 Third Avenue, near 39th Street

SHERMAN, WILLIAM TECUMSEH, STATUE, 14, 17
Fifth Avenue at 59th Street

SHIPS' CHANDLERS, 29
Eagle Bag and Burlap Company, 12 Fulton Street
See oilskin suits, rope, foghorns and seabags.

SIDEWALK CAFE, 26, 40
Fifth Avenue Hotel, Fifth Avenue and 9th Street
Also downtown are: The Cookery, Uni-

versity Place and 8th Street, and Longchamps, Fifth Avenue at 12th Street. (The Cookery is the least expensive.)

SIMON, KATE, 46

666 FIFTH AVENUE, 8

SMITH, AL, 45
Born in 1873, he worked as a boy in Fulton Fish Market. He was governor of New York and ran for President in 1928.

STOUFFER'S, 8

SPANISH-PORTUGUESE SYNAGOGUE CEMETERY, 26
West 11th Street, near Sixth Avenue
Opened in 1805, closed 1823, this is the second oldest (and very smallest) cemetery on the Island.

SUTTON PLACE, 30

THE STAGE, 22
834 Seventh Avenue, near 54th Street
This is a combination delicatessen and restaurant with sandwiches to eat there or to take out. It is open seven days a week 8 a.m. to 4 a.m.

STARK VALLA EMPORIUM, 26
109 West 10th Street, off Sixth Avenue
Gifts, old fashioned candies, nickelodeon that shows Charlie Chaplin for 5¢.

STATEN ISLAND FERRY, 31, 33,
Leaves from Battery Park.

STATUE OF LIBERTY, 35, 46
Liberty Island, New York harbor
Boats go on the hour 9 a.m. to 4 p.m. all year from Battery Park. Sculpted by Frederic Bartholdi, the statue was a gift to America from the people of France. Its base was donated by collections from American children.

STEUBEN, FRIEDRICH WILHELM, 44
This German officer volunteered to help Washington train his troops for the Revolutionary War. After the war he became a United States citizen and lived in the area now known as Yorkville on the east

side of New York. On Steuben Day, New Yorkers of German ancestry march up Fifth Avenue.

STEUBEN GLASS BUILDING, 8, 10
Fifth Avenue at 56th Street
Inside you can see, among other beautiful glass, the wedding present Eisenhower sent to the Queen of England. Outside the building, throw a coin in the pool. The money is collected daily and used to send city children to the country for vacations (the *Herald Tribune* is in charge of the program).

STORY TELLING AT CITY LIBRARIES, 41
For children from pre-school to 10 or 11 years old. For information call the main branch of the library and ask for the Children's Room.

STREET CAROUSEL, 40
A miniature carousel on a small truck wanders all over the Village in summer.

STUYVESANT, PETER, 42
This forceful governor of New Amsterdam built wharfs, cobblestone streets, and started the fire department. After the British took Manhattan he retired to his Bouwerie (farm) now called The Bowery.

STUYVESANT TOWN, 33
Built on site of former slums, this development houses 4,000 families.

TAKASHIMAYA, INC., 12
562 Fifth Avenue, 46th Street
New York branch of Tokyo's largest department store.

TEA CENTER, 10
16 East 56th Street
Stop for tea (free): a cup in winter, a cup or glass in summer.

TEAKWOOD HOUSE, 26
7 East 10th Street
Doors and trim for this house were imported from India.

TEMPLE EMANU-EL, REFORM, 17
Fifth Avenue at 65th Street

TENNIS COURTS, SOUTH MEADOW, 18
Central Park, near West 96th Street
Open April to last week in November, 8 a.m. to sunset. Players under 18 need a Junior Permit ($3.50). It may be obtained from the Borough Office, 64th Street and Fifth Avenue, Room 204.

TIFFANY'S, 10
727 Fifth Avenue, 57th Street
Your silver baby mug probably came from here. The biggest, finest, canary diamond in the world is on display.

TIME AND LIFE BUILDING, 20, 22
50th Street and Sixth Avenue
Changing exhibits in the street floor reception center are open weekdays 9 a.m. to 5 p.m.; Sundays, Mondays and holidays 11 a.m. to 6:30 p.m.

TIMES SQUARE, 22
Broadway and 42nd Street

TOM THUMB LOCOMOTIVE, 45
Designed by Peter Cooper in 1830, it was the first steam engine. Similar ones were used on city's street railways.

TOWN HOUSES, 16, 23
Look for them. They may be replaced soon by giant apartment houses. Now on the ground floors you can sometimes see a cook or the children of the house.

TRIBOROUGH BRIDGE, 34
Connects 125th Street, Manhattan; Hoyt Avenue, Astoria, Queens; and Bruckner Boulevard, The Bronx
Walk across if you have time. It gives a fine view of skylines, upper East River and the Harlem River.

TRINITY CHURCH, P.E., 25, 29
Broad and Wall Streets
Queen Anne gave the parish a grant of land in 1627. It is the parent Episcopal church of the United States.

TWIN PEAKS AND OLD FRAME HOUSE, 27
Grove and Bedford Streets
The Frame House is a remnant of the country village that once occupied this area. Behind it on Bedford there were once slave quarters. Twin Peaks was remodeled on Nuremberg lines by Otto Kahn.

UNION CARBIDE BUILDING, 23
270 Park Avenue, 47th Street
Visual exhibits of the atom and the story of uranium from mine to its use as fuel for nuclear reactors; open Monday through Friday from 9 a.m. to 6 p.m.; Saturdays 10 a.m. to 5 p.m. Closed Sundays.

UNITED NATIONS BUILDINGS, 9, 21, 23, 33
First Avenue from 42nd to 48th Streets
Open 9 a.m. to 6 p.m. Take a guided tour to find places to revisit at leisure. Tickets to various meetings are available on a first-come-first-served basis one-half hour before meetings. Earphones translate the proceedings into the official languages of the organization. Don't miss the shops—they are an international bazaar.

UNITED STATES COAST GUARD, 35
1 Bay Street, Staten Island
If weather permits, visitors can climb aboard cutters, buoys, buoy tenders and the Coast Guards' 327's Saturdays, Sundays and holidays from 1 to 4 p.m. Request permission in a letter to the Base Commander, telling day you plan to visit and number of people in the party.

VANDERBILT, COMMODORE CORNELIUS, 43

VANDERBILT MANSION, 45
Fifth Avenue, East 57th to East 59th Streets
This red brick and white stone chateau was the scene of many elaborate balls in the 1890's. The house was built from 1881 to 1894 and torn down in 1927.

VERRAZZANO BRIDGE, 35
Will connect Belt Parkway, Brooklyn, and Cloves Lake Expressway, Staten Island, when completed in 1965.

VILLAGE PRESBYTERIAN AND BROTHERHOOD SYNAGOGUE, 26
143 West 13th Street

WALDORF FLAGS—WALDORF-ASTORIA HOTEL, 21, 23
Park Avenue, 49th Street
A sign by the Park Avenue door of this great hotel tells which country's flag is flying. Also, the Ladies' Rooms off the main lobby are a fine place to tidy up after a busy afternoon and before dinner. Many restaurants; many stores in lobby.

WALKER'S PETIT MUSEE, 10
16 West 58th Street
Antique jewelry; jeweled Easter eggs for your charm bracelet can be bought here.

WALLACHS' BROUGHAM
see "Christmas Events"

WALLACHS DOG BAR, 9, 12
Fifth Avenue, 46th Street
New Yorkers know it's spring when the Dog Bar has water in it.

WASHINGTON ARCH AND WASHINGTON SQUARE PARK, 24, 27, 37, 43
Beginning of Fifth Avenue below 8th Street
Washington Arch was designed by Stanford White.

WASHINGTON'S INAUGURATION, 45
The country's first President was sworn into office in New York on April 30, 1789, at Federal Hall on Wall Street at Nassau.

WASHINGTON MEWS, 24, 26
Off Fifth Avenue between Washington Square North (Waverly Place) and 8th Street
Once an alley of stables for houses on the Square, it is now a row of lovely private houses.

WASHINGTON, GEORGE, STATUE, 25
Federal Hall National Memorial, Wall and Nassau Streets
Site of old Federal Hall where Washington was inaugurated.

WEBSTER, DANIEL, STATUE, 16
Central Park, off West Drive near 71st Street

WHITNEY MUSEUM OF AMERICAN ART, 11
22 West 54th Street
Contemporary American art on exhibit.

WOLLMAN MEMORIAL RINK, 17, 37, 41
Central Park, between East and Center Drive about 62nd Street
Ice skating mid-October to mid-April. The rink is open Sunday through Friday 10 a.m. to 1 p.m.; 2:30 to 5:30 p.m.; 8:30 to 11 p.m. Saturdays and school holidays from 10 a.m. to 12 N. children under 14 are admitted free; other sessions same as on other days.

WORLD'S FAIR, 35
Flushing Meadow Park, Flushing, Queens

WORLD SERIES, 37, 41
Yankee Stadium is host to these games in October — when the Yankees win the pennant!

YANKEE STADIUM, 34
161st Street and River Avenue, The Bronx
IRT Seventh Avenue or IND "D" train subways. Baseball games April to October. Professional football games from September to January. See newspapers for dates.

ZENGER, JOHN PETER, 45
He was editor of the *New York Weekly Journal* from 1733 to 1746. He wrote against city corruption and was brought to trial for libel against a crown officer, but was acquitted. His trial was one of the first victories for freedom of the press in the American colonies.

ZOO SHOP, 27
45 Christopher Street, near Sheridan Square
Toy and stuffed animals; also dolls and doll wardrobes.